DARE TO THINK IF YOU CAN

Think NOW for Growth and Happiness

Dare to Think if You Can
By **Sirshree** Tejparkhi

Copyright © Tejgyan Global Foundation
All Rights Reserved 2020

Tejgyan Global Foundation is a charitable organization
with its headquarters in Pune, India.

ISBN : 978-81-8415-719-2

Published by WOW Publishings Pvt. Ltd., India

First edition published in December 2020

First reprint in December 2022

Printed and bound by Trinity Academy, Pune, INDIA

Based on the Hindi book titled "Soch sako to soch lo" by Sirshree Tejparkhi

Copyright and publishing rights are vested exclusively with WOW Publishings Pvt. Ltd. This book is sold subject to the condition that it shall not by way of trade or otherwise, be lent, resold, hired out, or otherwise circulated without the publisher's prior written consent in any form of binding or cover other than that in which it is published and without a similar condition including this condition being imposed on the subsequent purchaser and without limiting the rights under copyright reserved above, no part of this publication may be reproduced, stored in or introduced into a retrieval system, or transmitted, in any form, or by any means, electronic, mechanical, photocopying, recording or otherwise, without the prior written permission of both the copyright owner and the above-mentioned publisher of this book. Any person who does any unauthorized act in relation to this publication may be liable to criminal prosecution and civil claims for damages.

Although the author and publisher have made every effort to ensure accuracy of content in this book, they hereby disclaim any liability to any party for any loss, damage, or disruption caused by errors or omissions, resulting from negligence, accident, or any other cause. Readers are advised to take full responsibility to exercise discretion in understanding and applying the content of this book.

*To those,
who contemplate and improve themselves,
and are prepared to bring change in themselves
for the purpose of Divine expression.*

Contents

	Preface	7
1.	Gather What You Have Scattered	11
2.	Delayed Gratification	15
3.	Unburden Yourself	19
4.	Become Aware of the Reality	23
5.	Extinguish the Fire of Envy - 1	28
6.	Extinguish the Fire of Envy - 2	33
7.	Round-up Your Bad Feelings	37
8.	Round-up the Wrong Responses	42
9.	Overcome the Quagmire of the Mind	46
10.	Learn to Choose Happiness	50
11.	Round-up Unsolicited Words	55
12.	Round-up Ignorance and Raise Awarenes	60
13.	Round-up Expectations of Help	64
14.	Round-up the Ego	68

15.	Deceit is a Disease	72
16.	Round-up Miserliness	77
17.	Negligence is a Disease	83
18.	Accept Your Parcels	86
19.	Round-up Acquisition and Preservation	91
20.	Round-up Your Fears and Tendencies	94
21.	The Art of Contemplation	99

PREFACE

Dare to Think NOW

An apprentice woodcutter was being trained by his supervisor. The supervisor assigned him an area in the woods and gave him an axe.

On the first day, the young woodcutter felled six trees. The supervisor congratulated him and asked him to keep going.

The woodcutter was motivated by the supervisor's words and tried harder the next day, but to his dismay, he could only cut four trees. On the third day, his performance dropped to two.

He couldn't understand why his performance was slumping. He lost his confidence; as a result his energy was sapped by negative thoughts. "Am I losing my strength? Will I lose my job?" the woodcutter wondered.

He went to the supervisor and admitted that he couldn't understand why his performance was going down.

"Have you sharpened your axe?" the supervisor asked.

"I didn't have the time to sharpen my axe. I've been busy chopping the trees…."

This is a famous story that carries an important message. The question we should ask ourselves is: Are we sharpening our axe? Or are we just too busy with our daily life?

Every New Year beckons us to ask: Have I explored all the possibilities that lie dormant within me? To answer this question, we need to identify whatever is incomplete within us. If we lack the feeling of fulfillment in certain areas of life, what can we do to attain completeness?

Completeness is experienced only when we choose to be creative instead of being reactive. For this, we need to throw light on our past conditioning—our prejudices, limiting beliefs, and burdens of the past. This is possible only through persistent self-observation and introspection. We need to harness and direct our thinking inward.

Thinking is an art. It is the key to tap into our limitless potential. Most people feel that thinking is a natural and spontaneous process. But we can achieve wondrous results by directing our thoughts inward through guided contemplation.

We need to make up our mind NOW: Do we continue to plod reactively through an ordinary life? Or do we DARE to think anew? Are we prepared to work on ourselves, to become our own sculptor? Can we train our mind for deep contemplation?

This book will make you contemplate your life. Every chapter has some questions at the end that will help you contemplate. Contemplate over these questions to eliminate any dark areas in your understanding and attain perfection in the key facets of your life.

While reading this book, you need to contemplate wholeheartedly without holding any reservations. The mind will try everything it can to avoid this process, but you need to quiet the mind and persevere. Contemplating on certain sensitive topics could bring up some deeply hidden weaknesses or negative feelings. The mind could possibly give up contemplation before we have dug deep enough and fully understood the topic. It may give excuses like, "That's a lot of contemplation for now. It is quite enough." However, when the mind does this, it is an indication for you to push yourself further, undeterred. It is then that deeper profound aspects of your life get revealed.

Allow this book to serve you and open a new chapter in your life. Read and reflect on each chapter to throw light on your life. This book will then precipitate positive changes in your life. May this introspection lead to a new dawn in your life!

1

Gather What You Have Scattered

We are All Collection Agents

A collection agent is someone whose job is to go about collecting debts that are pending recovery. His job remains incomplete until he has gathered everything that he has set out to collect. It is only when he has completed his task perfectly that he can rest peacefully.

But why are we discussing a collector's job?

This is because we too are performing the role of a collection agent in our life. We too are looking to gather and round-up something to feel complete and fulfilled—without which we cannot be at ease. Think, if you can!

We have descended on Earth to perform two kinds of collections: one, to collect some lessons, and two, to gather and round-up all the things that we have scattered in life.

The first kind of collection, for which we have undertaken this earthly journey, is to learn certain lessons in our life. Until we learn our lessons, a constant feeling of incompleteness and void constantly tugs at us; something keeps flaring up, a sense of being drawn. Some wish or an incomplete desire keeps arising, creating restlessness within us.

For example, if a person's lesson in life is patience, he would be constantly surrounded by people and situations that repeatedly provoke or agitate him. They would instigate him to lose his temper and give harsh, unwarranted responses. At such times, the person needs to learn to maintain his calm and be patient. The person being surrounded by provoking elements is a part of an immaculate arrangement made for him to learn his lessons.

Until we learn our lessons on earth, we will continue to feel incomplete and restless. As soon as we learn our lessons and develop the relevant virtues, our behavior gets transformed, and so does the arrangement around us. It is for this reason that it is said: "When we are unmoved by situations, situations move." A better way of putting it would be: "When our resolution to learn our lessons from the situation is unmoved, the situation moves on."

With this learning, we complete the first type of collection.

In the second type of collection, we set out to gather everything that we have transmitted. We collect all that we have scattered due to our tendencies and behavioral patterns. We need to round-up the baggage of wrong responses that we have given; we need to receive the payback for our past actions gracefully. Whether our actions were inspired by positive feelings, or by fear, greed, anger, or any other negative emotion, these are things that we have scattered far and wide, which we need to round-up.

By failing to do so, we will continue to remain caught up and deviate from the real purpose of our life, thereby leading a dissatisfied and unsettled life.

How do we begin this task?

The first step would be to contemplate and find out what all we have scattered in the first place, analyze the various areas of our life, and find out what we have to gather. And that is precisely what this book will help us achieve.

This book covers many areas that form the crux of our life, wherein we often get entangled. Guidance in these areas has also been provided, besides the pertinent questions on which we need to contemplate. This will help throw light on every aspect of our life.

Once we have completed the collection, our life will be full of peace and satisfaction. We will break free from dependencies like, "He should love me," "She should respect me," or "They should give me attention". We will no longer depend on others to feel happy and content. If we do receive love, attention, and respect from others, that's a bonus. But the eternal source of love, compassion, attention, and every positive emotion that lies within us, will be revealed. Even if people do not treat us well, our peace will remain unruffled.

People need not always behave well with us. They may act the way they want, but our perspective will have transformed and transcended these topics. Now, people may remain the same; their views and thoughts could still be the same, but we will have decided how we want to lead our life. Our life, thereafter, will not be based on expectations. Our peace and happiness will remain unaffected, regardless of how people behave. This is possible only when we have gathered back all that we have scattered!

Questions for Contemplation

1. What have you scattered so far, that you need to gather back? Write down your contemplation.

   _____

   _____

2. Once you have rounded-up all that you had scattered, how will your health, relationships, and life be?

   _____

   _____

3. What is your current state?
   a. Are your actions inspired by the desire to achieve something?
   b. Or are your actions inspired by the joy of having already achieved something?

2

Delayed Gratification

Freedom from the Need for Instant Gratification

Everyone seeks the experience of contentment, but this can only come with freedom from the need for instant gratification. We often act out of compulsion in a hurry to either satisfy our cravings or to escape something we have an aversion to.

Let us understand this with an example.

> There was a Brahmin couple who did not have children. The wife would often grieve over their childlessness. One day, the Brahmin brought home a mongoose for the wife's entertainment and to keep her mind off her sorrow. Slowly, the wife became fond of her pet mongoose and overcame her grief. She started feeling happy.
>
> A few days later, the Brahmin's wife conceived. Soon, the couple was blessed with a baby boy. Her happiness knew no bounds. She got so completely engrossed with her child that she started neglecting the mongoose. She *did* realize that she was wrong in doing so, but the happiness of having a child after so many years of marriage made her focus entirely on her newborn child.

One day, when she had put her son to sleep and had gone out to get water, a snake sneaked into the house. The mongoose caught sight of the snake and killed it before it could harm the child. The snake's blood was smeared on the floor and the mongoose's mouth.

The mongoose was overjoyed, thinking the Brahmin's wife would be happy about what he had done. He was delighted at the thought that she would appreciate him and finally pay attention to him as she did earlier. The mongoose waited impatiently for the Brahmin's wife at the entrance of the house with his blood-smeared face.

A little later, the Brahmin's wife returned with the pitcher of water. She noticed the mongoose with stains of blood on its mouth. She immediately concluded that the mongoose had harmed her child. In a fit of rage, she threw the pitcher at the poor mongoose, killing it on the spot.

Shivering with fear about what could have happened to her baby, the Brahmin's wife rushed inside the house only to find her child sleeping peacefully. She also saw the dead snake beside the cradle and understood what had transpired. She realized the grave mistake she had committed in her fit of rage.

After that day, the Brahmin's wife lived with the guilt of having killed the mongoose that had saved her child.

This is a famous story that we may have heard before. But what the story points out to us in this context is our need for instant gratification. Having seen the mongoose's mouth smeared with blood, the Brahmin's wife could not control herself because of her tendency to react impulsively. She immediately assumed the worst and ended up committing a grave mistake. This is what happens with most of us.

As soon as someone says something, we immediately react, often resorting to the use of hurtful words. We are consumed by the desire to get even. For some reason, if we cannot react in person, we send messages through the mobile. Most of us are unable to wait even for a day. Nowadays, it has become easy to get in touch with people, which unfortunately provides a faster way to vent our anger. We find it difficult to accept a delay in the fulfillment of our desires.

Very often, when our temper mellows down, we regret what we have said or done. We then feel, "It would have been better if I hadn't sent the message." Hence, it is better to delay the fulfillment of our immediate impulses rather than regretting later, because this is the only way to conquer the need for instant gratification. Those of us who find it difficult to overcome this need are left with no other option but to lead a life full of regrets and ruefulness.

To be free from the need for instant gratification, one needs to develop the quality of **delayed fulfillment**. In this age of order-at-our-fingertips, most people are deeply entangled in the habit of immediate satisfaction of their desires because of the systematic conditioning by advertisements on the television and the internet—instant home delivery, quick services delivered at the door, etc. Seeing or hearing these advertisements, people get into a frenzy for immediate fulfillment. To overcome these urges, we need to develop the quality of **delayed gratification**.

When you feel the need for something and are trying to acquire it, practice delayed fulfillment. You will choose to wait—for no particular reason—and delay receiving the thing. With the increasing practice of this behavior, you will observe how you begin to overcome the need for immediate gratification.

Imagine your favorite dish is kept in front of you, ready to be consumed, and you delay fulfillment by waiting for some time. Try this a few times; take it as a game in which you compete with yourself. When the competition is with yourself, the chances of winning are enhanced. Sometimes, you may win; at other times, you may give in to your desires, but do not stop playing. As you progress, you will learn how to win the fight with the trick of delayed fulfillment.

We try to develop qualities that are required to survive every day. But when we come to know about a new quality like delaying fulfillment, we get confused. We feel that delaying fulfillment is like sacrificing pleasure. But when we realize that this quality does not take any pleasure away from us, but instead gives us profound happiness and contentment, we then understand the importance of this quality.

There are many added advantages to this quality, but what is most important is its primary purpose. This quality can help us attain the highest goal of life—that of being established in the experience of the true Self. Hence, by overcoming our tendency of seeking instant gratification, we can lead a peaceful and satisfying life by developing the quality of delayed fulfillment.

Questions for contemplation

1. Contemplate your past actions that were based on the need for instant gratification, that you repent even today.

_____

_____

2. What steps do you intend to take, what changes do you intend to make from this moment onward to develop the quality of delayed fulfillment?

_____

_____

3. Analyze your past and current responses to situations that arouse feelings of unhappiness, anger, fear, or greed. Then, visualize how your response would be if you were to respond with delayed fulfillment? Write down your contemplation.

_____

_____

3

Unburden Yourself

Let go and Introspect

Two monks lived in a village. Every day they would cross a river that flowed on the outskirts to reach their monastery. Very often, when there was no boat available to cross the river, they would swim across.

One day, when they reached the banks of the river, they saw a lady waiting there. Upon enquiring, they found that the lady wished to cross the river but didn't know how to swim. She asked the monks to help her reach the other side. One of the monks agreed to carry her on his shoulders as he waded and swam across the river. A little while later, the two monks and the lady reached the other side of the river.

After some time, the monk who had carried the lady observed that the other monk was quiet. His face showed signs of anger. So, he asked him, "Why do you look angry, my brother?"

The other monk replied, "You agreed to carry the lady on your shoulders despite knowing that coming in direct contact with a lady does not fall within our principles. You have broken your vow of celibacy by doing this. Hence I am angry with you."

To this, the first monk replied, "I let go of the lady long back, but it seems you are still carrying her, albeit in your mind. Is it right to carry on with the burden in this manner?"

Fortunately, the other monk immediately realized his mistake and made amends, or else he would have carried this burden throughout his life.

There are two lessons to be learnt from this little story: one, **to let go,** and two, **to introspect.**

Letting go

The monk who had carried the lady was aware of the need of the hour—to help the lady, which he did. He moved on from his action after having left the lady at the riverbank. Due to his awareness and understanding, he did not burden himself with the thought, "*How can I carry a lady on my shoulders, being a monk?*" It was just another incident for him, which he was easily able to let go of.

The other monk was burdened with his thoughts about how his friend, despite being a monk, had carried the lady on his shoulders, thus breaching the sanctity of celibacy. His thoughts are an evidence of his narrow mindedness. Due to the lack of understanding, his thoughts made him restless. His friend's conduct gave rise to anger within him, which was a burden for him. However, when his friend explained his thoughts and perspective, he was able to let go of his burden.

Holding onto things is like punishing yourself long after things have happened and gotten buried in the past. A person may have wronged you once, but by holding on to the incident and the associated feeling, you are replaying the same thing in your mind repeatedly, punishing yourself several times for something that probably happened only once a long time ago. In such conditions, letting go becomes the oxygen that is desperately needed to save yourself from choking on to a thing of the past. We have to decide whether we want to live a life of burdens or that of freedom.

Introspecting

To introspect means to contemplate with the purpose of freeing oneself from mental burdens. Here, one needs to question oneself and seek the answer.

The first monk could have asked the other monk to contemplate the real cause of his displeasure. If the second monk had contemplated in the right direction, he could have been freed of the burden.

Everyone wants to be free of burdens that come with our worldly existence. But unless we contemplate the various incidents in our life with awareness, we continue to go about living mentally burdened and full of sorrow and resentment.

Instead of complaining and being despondent, we need to invest our time in seeking answers to questions such as:

- Why has this become a burden for me? What am I resisting?
- What thoughts, ideas, or assumptions am I unnecessarily carrying in my head that are making it difficult for me to accept the past?
- How long do I want to go about carrying the mental burden of incidents that have already occurred in the past, or that may occur in the future?
- Do I really want to be free from this burden?
- What steps can I take to unload this burden?

It is only by honestly seeking the answers to these questions within ourselves that we can be truly free from the unnecessary burdens we are carrying.

Questions for contemplation

1. Introspect over the mental burdens that you have been carrying till now.

   _____

   _____

2. Which mental burdens were you able to let go of after having gained an understanding of this topic? Write down your contemplation.

   _____

   _____

3. List the steps you intend to take to let go of the burdens you haven't yet released.

   a. _____

   b. _____

   c. _____

   d. _____

4

Become Aware of the Reality

Give Respect, Not Blame

A boy once had to undergo an emergency operation for which the doctor was called for urgently. As soon as the doctor reached the hospital, he began preparing for the surgery.

As he headed towards the operation theatre after the preparations, he met the boy's father. The father appeared troubled and worried. As soon as the father saw the doctor, he asked the doctor angrily, "Why did you take so long to come? Do you not know that my son's life is in danger? How can you be so irresponsible?!"

The doctor calmly replied, "I am sorry that I was not available at the hospital when I was informed about your son. Please excuse me and try to calm yourself down so that I may carry on with my job." To this, the father retorted, "Tell me doctor, had it been your son instead of mine, struggling to stay alive, would you have been so calm?" The doctor did not react to the father's words. He just said, "Doctors are not God. They only try to save the patient. I will try my best. You too can pray to God for your son."

After some hours, the doctor came out of the operation theatre looking quite satisfied. "Thank God", he said to the father, "the operation was successful, and your son is out of danger." Without waiting for the father's reply, the doctor started walking away. "If you have any queries, you may ask the nurse" he said as he left. The father thought, "How egoistic can he be?! Was it too much to ask for a few minutes? I would have asked him about my son's condition."

Later, when the father was speaking to the nurse, he voiced his thoughts about the doctor to her. The nurse replied, "You know, his son died in a road accident yesterday. When we contacted him for your son's surgery, he had gone to perform the last rites. But leaving that halfway, he came over to conduct your son's surgery and saved him. Having done that, he has gone back to complete the last rites."

Hearing this, the father felt ashamed and remorseful about his behavior.

The story teaches us that we should not indulge in blaming others, especially when we do not know the complete truth about any incident. We tend to draw judgments and form assumptions based on lies, imagination, and half-truths, and allow our thoughts to run amok.

People make assumptions and draw judgments without careful thought or understanding. They arrive at erroneous conclusions and then accuse others based on their biased findings or imaginations.

Let's say someone tells us that a certain other person is very arrogant and quarrelsome. On listening to this, we immediately create a mental image of the other person based on the description we receive, without realizing that it is just someone's opinion about the person. It could be untrue, but we borrow this opinion and presume it as the gospel truth without attempting to find the reality. The next time we come face to face with the person, we view him with the bias that we have already formed.

Often it so happens that the person is saying something, and we relate to it differently and make erroneous judgments. Such judgments weaken the mind, and a weak mind indulges in blaming. A weak mind is a sign of lack of awareness.

A mind with a lowered level of awareness blames others for whatever seems wrong. For such a mind, faults lie in the world, not within. "He is so rude. He couldn't take a minute to help me out," "I couldn't complete my task because she didn't complete hers on time," "Wealth has gone straight to his head," "People are so irresponsible on the road. That's why there's so much traffic jam these days," "He just doesn't love me anymore," and so on. All such thoughts demonstrate how people tend to blame others. But do they ever pause for a reality check? Facts are often different from our assumptions.

We can mature and progress in life only when we accept people and situations as they are, without painting them with our assumptions and judgments. Awareness and the acceptance of the truth leads to a blessed life. People who indulge in blaming always remain troubled because just as they refuse to accept others as they are, they also refuse to accept themselves. Guilt is nothing but blame that is directed inward.

Consider a person who makes false assumptions about his boss and keeps blaming him for everything. When you imagine this person in your mind, do you see a happy person or a grouchy one? Surely a grouchy one, who always remains troubled. Now imagine another person who accepts his boss as he is and has learnt to deal with him the right way. How does this person appear in your imagination? Happy, maybe not entirely contented but certainly less troubled than the first person.

People keep making false assumptions about others in their stupor. They need to remind themselves, "This is just a thought, an imaginary idea that has been created because of someone's words or my incomplete understanding. This is not necessarily the truth."

Every incident is a reminder of our true Self

Any incident, situation, or event, whether positive or negative, should serve the purpose of returning your attention to your divine consciousness; it should remind you of your true Self. The natural tendency of the mind during crisis is to try and pin the blame on someone or something else. This tendency has to be eliminated.

Contemplate sincerely on how long you want to carry the burden of blaming and finding faults in others. Think of what you are gaining from it. Think also of what you may be losing as a result. What are you trying to run away from by doing so? What are you trying to save yourself from? Is it your own desire to carry this burden? Introspect your state as clearly as you can, so that you know what corrective actions you need to take.

Someone illtreats us once and we continue to carry the burden of the insult for many years. We accumulate such experiences as if they are our wealth! We define ourselves in terms of such experiences, not realizing that it gives a wretched undertone to our life. But a time comes when we have to comb through our experiences and find out which ones are precious and which ones are unnecessary burdens.

Having contemplated and made up our mind about giving up the burdens, the next question is, "How do we let go of this burden? How do we make ourselves believe in our ability to let go of it?"

For this, we first need to work on ourselves. With sincere introspection, this can be easily achieved. We need to unburden ourselves of the negativity caused by the actions, words, and feelings of our family, neighbors, friends, bosses, and other acquaintances and enjoy the freedom that follows.

Remember that only we are responsible for our own happiness; no one else. When we are convinced about this, we will also happily take the responsibility of owning up situations we are in, without blaming others.

Questions for contemplation

1. In which situations do you tend to find faults in others because of your presumptions, without trying to find out the whole truth?

   _____

   _____

2. Contemplate your intention behind carrying the burden of blaming others. What steps do you plan to take to let go of this burden? Write down your contemplation.

   _____

   _____

5

Extinguish the Fire of Envy - 1

Recognize and Live Your Uniqueness

A sparrow saw an eagle soaring high, and thought to itself, "Why can't I fly so high?" Feeling depressed, it killed itself!

Have you ever heard of a bird or any other animal do this? Never. But with humans, this has almost become a new normal.

Students feel inferior when they compare their academics to that of others. Entrepreneurs feel depressed when they compare their business success with that of others. Others' success often lets a feeling of envious competition creep into peoples' minds. They are consumed by the fire of envious competition to such an extent that they cause themselves harm; they even go so far as to commit suicide.

When we compare ourselves or our situation with others, we forget that our understanding of the other person's situation could be wrong. It is possible that we only have a superficial understanding of others' lives. A person could be very wealthy, and we may envy him assuming that he has a perfect life; but that may not necessarily be true!

Unhealthy competition that arises from envy actually makes us unhappy at other's happiness. To compare someone's external state with our inner state, doesn't do any good. If we compare, we at least need to fully understand the other person's holistic state. Any comparison we make without doing this would be skewed and unjust towards ourselves and the other person.

In the same vein, if someone is asked about their inner state, they should be able to share the truth about it honestly. In the spree to project themselves as top-of-the-world, they suppress their unhappiness and further trouble themselves. It is for this reason that a great deal of importance is attached to sharing one's true feelings. Animals, birds, and other living creatures do not have this tendency to project what's not true. Their behavior is authentic. Let us understand this with an example:

> A crow was very unhappy about his complexion. His sorrow was further deepened when one day he saw a white duck. When the crow spoke to the duck about his fair complexion, he realized that the duck was unhappy about his complexion too!
>
> "I am only white!" said the duck, "Look at the parrot. How colorful it is! Why can't I look like that?!"
>
> The two then headed to the parrot and told her, "You are so lucky! You are blessed with beautiful colors."
>
> "I'm not so sure about my luck," the parrot replied, "I do not have as many colors as the peacock. Look at him... such beautiful colors! Why can't I look like that?!"
>
> Now, the three went to meet the peacock and praised him for his beauty. The peacock replied, "Yes, a lot of people come to see me and my beautiful colors, but except the crow, all other birds are kept in cages. If only I could fly free like a crow!"
>
> Hearing the peacock's words, realization dawned on the crow and he felt as if he had been washed white—from within. He was unburdened of the unnecessary comparison he was indulging in and his mind was purified by the understanding of his uniqueness. He came to know about the importance of his own original qualities that were envied by others!

This story demonstrates that each one has a unique skill, a unique talent, a natural flair. It lays dormant within until it is recognized, nurtured and allowed to bloom. A lot of people traverse through their life never discovering their originality. Their everyday struggle to earn a livelihood and keep up with competition keeps them so engrossed that the thought of realizing their natural talent never occurs to them. And that is quite understandable. It is not wrong to prioritize primary existential needs. However, one should also plan and explore oneself to identify at least one unique talent that they can offer to the world.

If a large part of your time is dedicated to earning a living, start by giving your unique talents a few hours every weekend. In this way, you accept and start *living* your uniqueness. Slowly it grows and fills your life to an extent that it can become your full-time occupation.

Observe the people whose job or profession involves doing things they love. Do they ever look tired? Do they feel like throwing it all away and escaping? No! Their work doesn't stress them. For them, their work is *pleasure*, not *effort*. It brings them a deep sense of satisfaction. What have they done differently? They realized their unique innate talents and nurtured them.

People who realize and harness their unique talents and originality tend to be happier and more peaceful than those who don't. Whatever comes naturally and effortlessly, is natural talent. A person may pick on a particular musical instrument faster than others. It is almost as if he was meant to learn it. That is his natural talent. Someone is innately good with numbers. Someone else enjoys studying people and their personalities. Someone finds the study of the human body and its workings fascinating. All these are inner callings.

If these people are able to make a career out of the natural talents of theirs, they have far better chances of leading a happier and stress-free life. On the other hand, people who ignore their calling or never realize what their calling is, end up living a life full of stress and dissatisfaction. A deep sense of unrest gnaws at them all the time.

The very first step to realize your natural talent is to stop comparing your life and situations to that of others. Only when the crow stops comparing itself to the duck, will it realize its uniqueness.

If you are clear about your calling, it will be the only thing that matters to you. In the story of the crow, the most important part was when the different birds spoke to each other. And what was furthermore crucial was that each bird frankly expressed its state honestly without falsely projecting that they were very happy! Had the duck said, "Yes, I am proud of my complexion!" instead of telling the truth, the crow would have ended up being unhappy all its life. However, it did not, and because the duck told the truth, the crow got a different and surprising perspective. When the crow finally realized his uniqueness, his external complexion didn't matter as he was washed white with pure happiness from within!

Likewise, whatever one's physical features are—dark, short, fat, thin, strong, weak, etc.—what matters is what is unique in them—their natural talent.

God, in His infinite wisdom and creativity, has created no two things exactly alike. Not even two leaves of a tree are alike; there is always some variation. This is God's creativity. Man is also a part of God's creation, and hence just like the leaves of a tree, no two people are exactly alike. There is always something unique about every person; the only need is to recognize it.

When we compare and compete with others, we tend to harbor jealousy and hatred towards them. Their progress makes us angry. It is very common for people to feel jealous when they see rich people. However, they fail to understand that by harboring negative feelings, they are causing themselves great harm. Their own negativity becomes the greatest roadblock to the prosperity that is waiting to flow in their life.

Instead of comparing our lives with others' and feeling jealous about their material possessions, we should seek inspiration in their qualities like confidence, health, love, happiness, and pray for those qualities.

In this manner, by discovering our unique calling, we can break free from the tendency to compare and find peace and satisfaction within.

Questions for contemplation

1. Contemplate the situations in which you compare or compete with others and become unhappy.

2. Are you able to honestly tell others the complete truth about your inner state? At times when you find it difficult to be honest, what stops you from being so?

3. When and for what reasons do you find yourself moving away from your natural calling? What steps can you take to re-align yourself?

6

Extinguish the Fire of Envy - 2

Share Your Blessings

We are getting to know how each person has an originality, a uniqueness that they can offer to the world. When we internalize this understanding, the tendency of comparing our life with that of others and feeling jealous naturally dissolves.

The only comparison that is justified is the one that we make with ourselves. We must constantly work on our natural talents and hone our skills. We should compare ourselves only with ourselves, by asking, "How can I do this task better than what I did yesterday?" This, and only this, is a worthy comparison, because it only brings improvement, not unhappiness.

Every person has desires about achieving goals and gaining wealth. But when things do not materialize according to their wishes, they feel unhappy. Furthermore, if they witness the fulfilment of the desires of people close to them, like a relative, friend or a neighbor, they feel even more miserable and jealous. So much that they even go to the extent of harming themselves and others.

Here's a story that underlines this tendency of people.

> There was once a person who pleased God through intense meditation and ascetic practices. Materializing before his eyes, God said, "Ask for whatever you wish, my child!"

The person thought for a few moments and replied, "O Lord, I want all my wishes to come true as long as I live!"

God smiled, "Alright my child. I bestow upon you this boon: as long as you walk the earth, all your wishes shall be fulfilled. However, there is one condition that you have to accept: whatever you ask for yourself, your poor and needy neighbor shall receive double!"

The person was surprised at this inexplicable condition, but the prospect of having every wish fulfilled for as long as he lived, filled him with joy and he thanked God profusely.

As days went by, the person noticed that indeed whatever he wished for, his neighbor received double. He wished for a large and luxurious home, his neighbor received a home twice as large and luxurious! He wished for money and gold and his neighbor received double the amount he got. He wished for fame and his neighbor became twice as famous as him!

He just couldn't take it anymore. The thought of his neighbor receiving more riches, luxuries, and fame than him, started poisoning his mind. Instead of feeling happy about what he had, he started feeling miserable about what his neighbor had gained.

Finally, one day, consumed by the fire of envy, he wished for the rupture of one of his own eyes, knowing that according to the boon, his neighbor would receive double of what he wished for, meaning the neighbor would lose both his eyes!

In this way, envy can make people harm not only themselves but others too. Something that was a great boon, something that could have been used to bring happiness and prosperity to oneself and to others, finally became a curse—all because of envy. Had he saved himself from the unnecessary comparison with his neighbor, he could have realized that he had more than enough for himself and stayed happy and content.

The boon granted to him by God was his uniqueness. Had he chosen to share it with people and help the poor and needy, he could have derived great sense of satisfaction while being a cause for a greater good. He could even have collaborated with his neighbor, discussed the situation with him, and induced him to give away the surplus that he received to the poor and needy as well. In this way, he could have got his neighbor to do charity alongside himself.

However, unfortunately he got caught in the fire of envy. His consciousness and actions spiraled down and he deprived not only himself but also his neighbor of happiness.

Just like the boon that was the uniqueness of the person in the story, every person on earth is blessed with a boon—a unique talent, a unique gift—that they can share with the world and be the cause of a greater good. All it takes is for them to recognize it, embrace it, develop it, and give it to the world. Not everyone may be capable of the kind of severe practice and penance that this person did, and yet everyone could have benefitted from that capability of his. In other words, he could have been the cause of financial upliftment for so many people, but unfortunately his envy turned the boon into a curse.

Let us introspect our lives to find out whether we have spread negativity out of envy and jealousy. Are we holding back our natural talent from blossoming into a beautiful flower, the sweet fragrance of which can express the divine qualities of love, joy and peace?

Questions for contemplation

1. Contemplate and write down all the instances since your childhood when you felt envy on comparing yourself or your life with someone else.

   _____

   _____

2. Introspect to discover your uniqueness. What natural talents do you possess? Which activities, tasks, or work do you find yourself innately good at?

   _____

   _____

3. Having discovered your unique talent(s), how can you utilize it (them) to benefit people, to solve their problems, to make their lives better, and in general, to make the world a better place?

   _____

   _____

7

Round-up Your Bad Feelings

Discover the Secret of Feeling Good

Let's say a friend of yours, who has just returned from a trip abroad, meets you. While describing his journey, he tells you, "Have you been to Switzerland? You have to go there if you haven't. The Swiss alpine vistas are spectacular! You will really feel good."

Have you ever wondered why people say that? What do they exactly mean by "feel good"? Why do we all have the desire to feel good?

Let us understand this in detail.

The secret of "feeling good"

People visit tourist places; they spend time there sightseeing, playing, and enjoying, and then return home feeling "good" about having seen a new place. They tell others about their experience, "We had an amazing time! You too should visit; you will feel good."

When people feel good doing something, they share their experience with their friends and family, asking them to do the same so that they may derive the same happiness that they did.

But taking out trips, visiting new places, tasting new dishes, buying new things, throwing parties, watching movies, etc. are all external reasons that make people feel good and refreshed. These activities keep their mind engaged for a short period and the resultant happiness seems to have come from the activity that was undertaken. But is that the truth? Are these activities the real source of happiness? Let us understand the secret of "feeling good."

We all like to feel good. Nearly every action is inspired by some desire, some goal—like the completion of a certain task, solving a certain problem, earning money, acquiring material things, and so on. To achieve these goals, we are prepared to do anything. Fulfillment of our goals makes us feel elated and their non-fulfillment fills us with despair.

However, when we understand the secret, we can feel good and happy anytime, without waiting for any external stimulus. When we stop depending for happiness on the fulfilment of our tasks, goals, our achievements, receiving love or appreciation, or acquiring material possessions, we will find the key to an eternal wellspring of pure divine bliss, which is accessible all the time.

On one hand, is a person who wins a lottery worth a thousand pounds and still feels sad because he desired to win a ten thousand pounds lottery. On the other hand, is a person who loses his wallet and is still happy that it contained only a few pound notes. He thinks from his heart, "Thank God, I wasn't carrying much cash! Whatever I have lost shall surely come back to me if it belongs to me. But whatever little money was there in the wallet, I hope it helps whoever it ends up with!"

Thinking thus, a person who would otherwise have felt sad about having lost something, feels happy and grateful because he thinks of the incident from his heart, not his judgmental head. In spite of having gained something and having a genuine reason to feel happy, the first person feels sad because he looks at the incident from his head, and his head tells him, "More is better, less isn't!"

We too need to round-up our negative feelings and learn to think from our heart. This is the key to feeling good and being happy in any eventuality: think from the heart, not the head.

There are matters that need to be dealt with from the head and those that need to be dealt with from the heart. The greatest roadblock in feeling good all the time is our own tendency to use our head when we should be using our heart. (Here, 'Heart' does not refer to the physical heart, but rather the very essence of our Being.)

We are now getting to know that we need to perceive every incident from our heart. We need not *wait* for things to happen, goals to be achieved, or tasks to be completed to feel good. Happiness, peace, love, abundance are our innate qualities. They are like the sun that is always present, but hidden behind the clouds, waiting for the clouds to disperse, so that its ever-present shine is visible again!

Everything changes when we decide to observe every incident from the heart. That is the secret to being happy all the time, to feeling freedom and fulfilment all the time, without any dependency on external factors.

'Good' things are the *w* of being happy, not the *cause*.

You can feel good and be happy anytime because it is the desire of your heart and the nature of the true Self. The same Universal Self desires to experience itself through different bodies. However, Self-realization is possible only in a body that is free from past conditioning. This is similar to you wanting to see yourself in the mirror, but which is only possible if the mirror is clean. In such a 'pure body-mind, the Self finds it easy to return to Self-experience. It is the desire of the Self that everyone should uninterruptedly feel good and happy all the time.

This answers the question why everyone wants to feel good; because it is the desire of the true Self.

Every stone can be a stepping-stone

In the journey of happiness, we get stuck at certain milestones that give us temporary relief and never proceed further to reach the destination of true happiness.

If a person, who is caught in quicksand, finds a stone, he tries to latch onto it to avoid sinking further. The stone temporarily delays his sinking, and so he continues to hold onto it. He could have used it as a stepping-stone to pull himself out. But out of ignorance and fear, he keeps holding onto the stone and never frees himself from the quicksand.

In much the same way, when stuck in the quicksand of sorrow, one gets temporary solace and relief from the 'bad feeling' by listening to sad songs, watching movies that depict tragedies, indulging in emotional eating, or receiving words of pity from people.

With the right understanding, we can use the 'bad feeling' or sorrow itself as a stepping-stone to pull ourselves out of its clutches. It is not wrong to seek relief, but by holding onto temporary reliefs thinking they are the only cures to our unhappiness, we cause ourselves great harm.

Every seemingly negative incident in our life occurs with the specific purpose of teaching us a lesson that we are here to learn. Hence, instead of looking for temporary relief from the situation, we need to contemplate on it, learn our lessons, and grow in maturity and resilience.

We need to strengthen our resolve to confront and overcome the 'bad feeling' instead of escaping it. When we look at the situation in the eye, we may experience some unease that comes from stepping out of our comfort zone. However, this unease is auspicious, as it comes as a prelude to a stronger and better version of ourselves.

With the internalization of this understanding will come the absolution from all bondage, freedom from sorrow, which will then catapult us to the experience of Self-realization and Self-abidance.

Questions to contemplate

1. What are the external factors your happiness has been dependent on till today?
   _____
   _____

2. Which are the tasks, goals, or achievements, the unfulfillment of which has made you feel unhappy? Pen down some instances:

   a. _____
   b. _____
   c. _____
   d. _____

3. As on today, what are the obstacles to 'feeling good' all the time?
   _____
   _____

4. What actions do you plan to take and changes you plan to make, to fulfill the desire of the true Self? Write down your contemplation.
   _____
   _____

8

Round-up the Wrong Responses

Be Happy to Create a Bright Future

There are four aspects to every incident that happens in life. By being aware and paying close attention to these four aspects, we can make the most of the occurrences in our life. Let us understand the four aspects.

The first aspect is *impact*.

As soon as an incident happens or someone says something to us, we are impacted by it. The incident, by itself, is actually neutral. However, when the incident impacts us, it triggers a programmed reaction based on our past conditioning.

This leads to the second aspect—*suffering*.

The impact of the incident on us manifests in the form of anger, irritation, hatred, jealousy, resentment, or contempt that we feel within us. These are our sufferings. Whenever we are troubled by someone or something, the understanding should be that nature is serving us the consequences of our own past actions through the person or the incident.

For example, if someone abuses you, you have to understand that those are your own abusive words, something that you have thought about or said to someone in your past, that have returned to you through the same or even a different person. What goes around, comes around. It is the law of karma. Knowing that it is your own behavior that is coming back to you will save you from feeling sad about others' behavior.

Also, the other person may have abused us only once, but we may be holding onto that memory and keep repeating it in our mind several times, thereby greatly intensifying our own suffering. Who then should be held responsible for our sufferings? The other person or we ourselves?!

Contemplating in this manner can absolve us of our tendency of inflicting sorrow on ourselves.

When we are unaware of how the impact of the incident triggers suffering within us, it leads to the third aspect—***reaction***.

The human tendency of giving an impulsive reaction would make us respond negatively to being abused or illtreated. In the heat of the moment, we forget that there are other possible responses that we can choose; hence we react based on our past conditioning. However, with awareness, we can break this tendency and respond positively and happily, regardless of the treatment meted out to us.

But why should we respond positively? The answer lies in the fourth aspect—***creation***.

By reacting to a negative incident or treatment in a similar manner, we unknowingly sow seeds of negativity for our own future. Every reaction we give is a seed that will create our future. To create a better future, we have to respond with awareness instead of reacting impulsively.

By focusing on these four aspects in any incident and responding with awareness and happiness, we will soon experience a bright future.

People go through several happy and unhappy incidents every day, but each one responds differently to situations and each response contributes to their future. A seemingly sad incident may not affect every person associated with it in the same way. There would be some who succumb to their past conditioning and feel sad, while there will also be some who become aware and choose a happy and loving response unconditionally. The latter are able to learn from such incidents and respond mature.

By choosing to respond happily to any incident, we are not only making the better choice for ourselves, but also giving the freedom of choice to the other person. If we react angrily, we may not leave the other person any choice other than reacting angrily.

The key to a happy future lies in the present. The seeds for a happy future are to be sown in the fertile soil of the present.

Going through the incident with awareness and giving a positive response will give you a feeling of victory because your response was not based on the other person's behavior, but on your understanding. You are not reacting but responding with happiness. Can there be a better victory than this?!

When you understand that reacting as they wish is the other person's right, you will be freed from the unhappiness due to others' behavior. When you give children the right to play mischief, you do not feel unhappy when they play mischief. Similarly, when you give the other person the right to behave as they wish, then you give yourself the freedom to choose to remain happy.

After receiving this understanding, in a seemingly unpleasant conversation with someone, you wouldn't say, "The other person said this." Instead, you would say, "The other person made the choice of saying this." You will not only choose to remain happy but will also choose to create your future. If the other person doesn't behave properly with you, you will still pray for him. You will be able to forgive him and yourself.

It is only by tiding through testing times that you realize that suffering is unnecessary. The option of staying happy is always available to you. If you choose to stay happy, you will beget a beautiful and successful future.

Questions for contemplation

1. Contemplate on how the negative incidents in your life have impacted you.

   _____

   _____

2. How have you reacted to negative incidents? How are your responses today?

   _____

   _____

3. Based on the understanding from this chapter, what specific steps will you take to create a beautiful future for yourself?

   _____

   _____

9

Overcome the Quagmire of the Mind
Enhance its qualities

Negative thoughts and responses cause emotions like fear, anger, jealousy, and greed. When we harbor these emotions for an extended period of time, they turn the mind into a quagmire of sadness and restlessness.

The specific purpose of using the metaphor of a quagmire is that a person who gets stuck in a quagmire finds himself being sucked down. The harder he kicks and struggles to save himself, the deeper he is sucked. Likewise, an afflicted mind goes down a spiral of sadness and depression, unless it is properly dealt with.

But how do we deal with such a mind?

There are some very important aspects we need to understand before we begin working on the mind to cure it of the quagmire.

To begin with, we have to get the mind into a receptive state because only a receptive mind has the ability to comprehend, understand, and assimilate. Our mind becomes receptive when we pray. So, the very first thing to do is to pray for the dissolution of the mind's tendencies so that it can be free from unhappiness.

Observe your mind

There is a specific goal for which we all have descended on earth—to realize the experience of who-we-truly-are. The greatest roadblock in achieving this purpose are the self-sabotaging tendencies of the mind. To dissolve these tendencies, we have to begin by observing them. Watching the thoughts, responses, and emotions of the mind in the light of awareness starts the process of dissolving them, thus purifying the mind.

Consider the example of a child's mind. It is innately pure and untarnished by negative tendencies. When the child is taken to a bath or a pool, it is not afraid of the water or worried about drowning. It enjoys the experience of floating in the water. But do grown-ups behave the same way? An adult's mind will have a flurry of thoughts and emotions. Most adults, who don't know swimming, will be afraid of entering the pool, thinking, "I can't swim. I will drown!"

To learn to swim, one has to train oneself. Likewise, one has to train oneself to observe the tendencies of the mind and stay afloat in the ocean of worldly and material distractions. To understand the true Self, one has to first understand how the mind works; one has to well and truly observe it. To annihilate the false beliefs and assumptions, the mind needs to be observed in the light of awareness.

Importance of the qualities of the mind

Let us understand the qualities of the mind with an example. There was once a frog that was trained to jump whenever someone said "Jump." If one of the four legs of the frog were to be cut, the frog would still jump upon hearing "Jump". If two of its legs were to be cut, it would still at least try to jump. However, if its third leg were to be cut as well, it will not be able to jump at all.

In such a scenario, if someone were to draw the conclusion that "cutting its third leg causes the frog to become deaf", it would be a joke! Someone can form such an incoherent inference instead of understanding that the frog is unable to jump because it has lost three legs.

Absurd as this may seem, such is the stupidity of the untrained mind! An untrained mind will always draw erroneous conclusions and stay entangled in false beliefs. A trained mind analyzes things from all perspectives in the light of awareness, saves itself from the mire of delusion, and finally plays an instrumental role in the attainment of Self-realization.

To train the mind, it is necessary to listen, read, contemplate the Truth, and meditate. This helps sharpen the mind and hone its abilities.

Observing as if for the last time

Let's say you were taken to your car or your bike and were told that you are seeing it for the last time. How would you look at it?

Imagine you are sweating, and you are told, "Observe yourself as you sweat. You will never sweat after today." Consider how deep and concentrated your observation will be as you perceive each and every drop of sweat that forms and rolls down your skin.

Now apply the same situation to your tendencies and negative emotions. Watch them, as they arise, as if you are going to experience them for the last time. Observing your sorrow or anger in this manner, takes away its ability to make you feel low. This is because you observe the emotion or tendency with detachment, without getting consumed by it. The emotion or tendency loses its power to distract you from being in your true nature of inherent joy and peace.

Continued practice of relentless observation will lead to the development of the quality of being able to observe emotions and tendencies without getting attached or distracted by them. We begin to realize that our every attempt to escape our negative emotions was futile. The more we resist the quicksand, the faster we get sucked into it. We never needed to escape unhappiness at all! Its dissolution was staring us in the face all the time. With the timely introspection of our emotions and tendencies, a transformation will take place.

A rocket has to exert a lot of energy to exit the earth's gravitational influence, but once it is out, its movement is almost effortless. Thereafter, it has to spend very less energy to reach its destination. Similarly, you have to exert a lot of effort to free your mind from the effect of its emotions and tendencies, but once it is freed, the journey to Self-realization is smooth and effortless.

Questions for contemplation

1. Contemplate and write down the emotions and tendencies that delude you most often.
   _____
   _____

2. Observe yourself to identify the situations in which you get entangled in the quagmire of the mind? What can you do to free yourself?
   _____
   _____

3. What steps do you plan to take to enhance the qualities of your mind and destroy its tendencies?
   _____
   _____

10

Learn to Choose Happiness
Let go of the Habit of Choosing to Suffer

A person once visited a temple. As was the custom, he left his footwear at the gates while entering, but when he returned, he found them missing. Realizing that his footwear had been stolen, he got very angry and started cursing. After a few minutes of intense ranting, he took off from the temple, wearing someone else's footwear!

In his unawareness, he sowed the seeds of unhappiness for his own future by the use of foul language and stealing.

This example underlines some common tendencies of the mind. Such trivial incidents occur almost daily and arouse feelings of anger, hatred, and resentment in us. The moment the incident occurs, we resist both, the incident itself and the associated emotions by thinking, "Why did this have to happen to me? Why do I have to suffer this way?"

It is true that we have no control over what happens. But as we have discussed in the earlier chapter, what we do have control over is how we respond to whatever happens. Our choice, and nothing else, determines whether what happened was a boon or a curse. Incidents keep repeating in life till we learn to respond in the right way.

Once we listen to a joke and have a good laugh, we seldom laugh as much as we did the first time when the same joke is repeated. If the ability of something to induce laughter and happiness decreases over time, why doesn't the ability to induce unhappiness also wane with time? Why do similar instances repeatedly make us unhappy, and not just as unhappy as the previous time, but even more!

This is because we resist what has happened instead of accepting it. Incidents repeatedly occur when we fail to learn the lesson, they have for us. When we are determined to accept incidents as they are, contemplate, and learn from them, we begin to turn curses into boons. We begin to make the choice of responding from a place of happiness.

Different people treat us differently every day based on their level of awareness and state of mind. We keep getting bothered and troubled by their deeds. Whenever we meet someone or speak to them, it is like giving the remote control of our happiness in their hands! There are several people we have to interact with every day: we have to work with them, speak to them, live and eat with them, do business with them. And each person behaves according to their present state of mind, which we will have almost no control over. If we were to base our happiness on the treatment meted out to us by so many people, we're almost guaranteeing that we will never be happy!

It is time to grab the remote control of our happiness back from others' hands. We have to cure the habit of choosing to suffer, be decidedly happy, and respond from a happy state of mind. We need to decide how we want our life to be. We cannot dodge incidents but can resolve not to be negatively affected by them.

Contemplate on the following questions:

Question 1: What is it that should reduce, but keeps increasing? What is it that should increase, but keeps reducing?

Question 2: When an incident occurs, are you in a hurry to be happy or unhappy?

People impulsively choose suffering over happiness as they do not have the understanding and the skill to convert a curse into a blessing. It even appeals to their logic: "How can I be happy when I have just lost my wallet?!"

This is the result of years of negative training and conditioning we have received since our childhood for being unhappy whenever an adverse incident occurs. This conditioning has now become a tendency; it has seeped into our subconscious mind, making us choose unhappiness every time.

Reflect sincerely: When someone's behavior troubles me, why am I in a hurry to feel unhappy? Why don't I choose to be happy?"

You will find that in unawareness, you always choose to be unhappy. Even then, if you can ask yourself, "How do I want my mood to be? No matter how people behave, whatever be the atmosphere, how do I want to feel?" With this conscious questioning comes the freedom of choice and you will notice that you start feeling better in the same situations that used to trouble you earlier.

In a race, the runners stand at their starting positions, and as soon as the gunshot is heard, they start sprinting towards the finish line. In life too, we are always running some race to hit the finish line. And why do we run races? Because reaching the finish line and winning the race gives us happiness and satisfaction.

With this in mind, can we make a little change to the way we participate in the race of life? Can we shift the finish line to the point from where we *begin* racing?!

Think about it: at the very outset of the race, we have already crossed the finish line! So, the purpose of the race—to be happy—is already achieved. Now we are not running the race *to get* happiness, but because we *are* already happy! The goal is already achieved even before we start running. This way we even enjoy the activity of running better because we are a happy runner! Imagine if we were told at the very beginning of the race that we have already won! What pleasant joy would it be to run!

Every action of ours across the day, week, year, and life is inspired by the need to be happy. What if we began with the finish line?

Let us make our happiness the *source* of our actions and not the *target*.

When someone treats us in a way that makes us unhappy, we are not aware of the reasons why the person chooses to do so. We are not well acquainted with their state of mind. However, what we do have control over is how we respond to them and how we choose to feel within.

If happiness is what we finally want to finish with, let's bring it to the starting line. Let's decide to be happy upfront, regardless of how incidents unfold. Choosing happiness breaks our tendency of rushing into unhappiness as soon as an incident occurs. We take a pause after the incident, during which we exercise our freedom of choice.

With this understanding, we can live a worry-free and unconditionally happy life in which every action *begins* from the finish line!

Questions for contemplation:

1. Contemplate your responses to people and incidents in your life so far.
   _____
   _____

2. Contemplate and write, how your mood changes in undesirable incidents.
   _____
   _____

3. Contemplate and write down the steps you plan to take to turn incidents into blessings.
   _____
   _____

11

Round-up Unsolicited Words

Be Wise, Not 'Literal'

Our life is shaped by the words we utter every day. We like to speak to someone who always uses sweet, polite, respectful and positive words. If we were to make courteous and positive talk a habit, the power of our speech would be greatly enhanced. It is entirely up to us to choose how we want to communicate with people.

There are certain tribes where people kill or wound by shooting poisoned darts. The negative and abusive words we speak are like these poisoned darts. They may cause great harm to whomever we say those words; they could even cause death.

It is hence imperative for us to be mindful of what we say and what we hear. Some negative words or sentences we chance upon, might percolate within and cause great harm. Words and the associated emotions can percolate so deep that they are remembered for several years. Things that people hear in their childhood affect them even in their adulthood. It is hence very important to specially pay attention to the power of the tongue and the ears. We need to train them so that they do not cause harm to others; instead, they should inspire them and induce positive feelings in them.

Hurtful words cause 'double losses'

Though it may not sound very important to many of us, we have to be highly aware of every word we speak, because we can be sure that it will come back to us someday. Most of us have fallen into the habit of casually using negative, abusive, or teasing words in our speech. We fail to understand that something that we may be saying casually or even unknowingly, can affect someone very deeply. They may have heard the same words in their childhood from someone who may have been angry. For this reason, those specific words and their past emotions could be still hurting them deep within. When we use the same words with them, their emotional pain is refreshed. Words affect different people in different ways because of their past experiences.

For example, let's say a person who has a hereditary condition of having very thin hair on his head has been teased about 'being bald' since his childhood. He has grown up being mocked about his physical appearance. This becomes a deep wound. Later, even in his adulthood, when a friend repeats the same mocking words, he would feel just as hurt and depressed, although he may not show it on the face. The friend who mocks him not only sows negative seeds for himself, but also causes his friend to feel hurt over something that he already had negative emotions about. This becomes a double loss—both the people involved in this conversation are negatively impacted. In this case, the person who mocks his friend about his baldness may be unaware of the trouble he has had to undergo in his past. He chooses hurtful words out of ignorance But, at the least, the friend can mindfully choose how he receives the words and responds to them.

Whenever we are on the receiving end of hurtful words from someone, we should ask ourselves, "Had they not said those hurtful words, how would I be feeling right now?" Asking ourselves this question immediately makes us aware of our inner state and shifts our focus from suffering to happiness. With practice, this can become a natural reflex; others' hurtful words will roll off like water rolls off a waxed surface. This reflexive awareness gives us the freedom to choose the words that we want to let in.

Breaking the Chain Reaction

When one person ill-treats another or says hurtful words, the speaker may not be able to grasp the impact of his negative words on the listener. Hurt by the words and feeling unhappy, the listener feels the need to vent his frustration and anger on someone else. Consequently, the effect of the words spoken by one person starts a chain reaction that impacts several people. The person who vents his anger and frustration walks off feeling a little better, but the recipient is now filled with frustration and on the lookout for someone else to unload it on. This chain has to be broken somewhere. And it can be broken only by someone with awareness, who responds to the situation differently than all the others in the chain.

The chain of frustration breaks when it encounters a person who:

- Allows the emotion to play out without affecting him;
- Seeks forgiveness for the speaker, and also forgives him for his words and actions;
- Takes a pause to be in meditation and watches the whole episode without being attached to the story.

As the number of people with this ability increases, the chain of frustration and anger will reduce.

Not only should we mindfully avoid indulging in gossip, backbiting, or negative criticism, but also try to be instrumental for others' mental stability and spiritual growth.

Be wise, not 'literal'

Words have immense power. They have the potential to unite people. But for that to happen, we have to first realize the potential of words and their impact on different people. Not every person who listens is the same: some are 'literal', and some are wise.

'Literal' people are those who always take the literal meaning of words that are said to them. Such people attach a lot of importance to spoken words and they are greatly affected by them. Material losses or physical harm caused by others may not affect them as much as others' words do. They are unable to accept improper words and can keep brooding over them for days on end. They are often unable to understand the feelings or intentions behind those words.

On the other hand, the wise do not get entangled in people's words. They are able to go beyond the words and understand the emotion and state of mind of the people that the words are coming from. If someone were to ill-treat them in his anger, they are able to respond with understanding and give him the benefit of doubt. They can see through the feelings and intentions behind words. Hence, they realize that the other person has spoken impulsively; that he didn't really mean it.

It must be clear by now that being wise, and not 'literal', should be our aim. Let us begin rounding up the unsolicited, negative, hurtful words that we say to people, causing them unhappiness. Let us learn to choose happiness, regardless of whatever words we hear or treatment we receive. Furthermore, let us learn to respond to incidents and words in a way so as to bring happiness and satisfaction to others.

Having understood what has been discussed in this chapter, contemplate the questions given below so that there remains no part of your life that gives you unhappiness.

Questions for contemplation

1. Contemplate on the specific words that have a negative impact on your state of mind.

   _____
   _____

2. Contemplate and write down the words that you are in the habit of using frequently, that could possibly affect others negatively. Which positive words can you replace them with?

   _____
   _____

3. Contemplate and pen down how you can sweeten your speech and develop the spirit of forgiveness?

   _____
   _____

4. How do you plan to develop reflexive awareness for negative words?

   _____
   _____

12

Round-up Ignorance and Raise Awareness

Watch Your Thoughts

There is a well-known story of two donkeys. Let us look at the story in the light of how it applies to the context of awareness.

> Two donkeys were walking alongside each other, each one carrying the load that their owner had placed on their back. One donkey carried a sack containing ten kilograms of salt, and the other carried ten kilograms of cotton. Although both the loads were similar in weight, the sack of cotton appeared larger.
>
> The donkey carrying the sack of cotton kept feeling sad thinking that it was carrying more burden than the other. It kept telling the other donkey, "The owner has put more burden on my back. Look at the size of the sack!"

Did the donkey really have any reason to fret? Had it known that irrespective of the size, the weight it was carrying was the same as what the other donkey was carrying, he might not have been so unhappy.

The same is true for us too. Most people remain unhappy by constantly fretting and overthinking about things that they need not. People often do this all their life! Their thoughts become an unnecessary burden that they carry throughout their lives. They assume the illusory truth (incidents of their lives that they have perceived negatively) to be the reality. They curse their luck for sending only hardships and troubles their way and continue to be unhappy. It may sound nonsensical, but this unhappiness becomes their comfort zone! They find solace dwelling in sorrow and self-pity.

Let us return to the story and see what happened with the donkeys thereafter:

> As it was getting very hot in the afternoon sun, the donkey carrying the salt went and sat in a pool of water. As it settled into the cold water, some of the salt in the jute bag dissolved in the water. A few minutes later, when the donkey got up to leave, it felt surprised that the load on its back had reduced all of a sudden.
>
> The donkey went and shared this with the other donkey, "Hey... you know what? Looks like this pool has magical water! I just sat in it a few minutes ago, and when I got up, my load was reduced."
>
> The other donkey, also wanting to get rid of its burden, went and sat in the water. But lo and behold! Instead of reducing, its burden became heavier because the cotton got soaked in water. The donkey returned from the pool, unhappier than before!

Like the donkey, some people try to imitate others' actions without applying their own logic and understanding, in the hope of getting the same results. But when things go wrong, they feel even more miserable.

We may have heard people complaining, "Why did this have to happen to me of all people?!" They do this because they are unknowingly comparing themselves with others, overindulging in thoughts of misery, jealousy, envy, hatred, thus inviting sorrow.

Remember that each person's life situations are unique. Instead of obsessing about what others are doing with their lives, we should focus only on that which we are required to do. We have to learn to control our thoughts and keep them from running amok.

The best way to rein in our thoughts is to practice watching our thoughts. Simply sit and watch your thoughts like a railway station guard, who watches trains pass by the station. When we learn to control our thoughts, their control on us starts reducing. They lose the ability to consume our energy.

Thoughts can only control us when we are unaware of them; our indulgence in them causes unhappiness. Unhappiness, in turn, deepens our unawareness, thus creating a vicious cycle. The remedy to this is awareness.

Thoughts are like flares that arise in the night sky, shine for an instant, and then fade away. Thoughts arise in the sky of our awareness and then dissolve. Just as we enjoy the dazzling display of flares during fireworks, we can enjoy the display of thoughts, regardless of what the thoughts are saying. For this, we need to learn to witness the thoughts as just thoughts, and not what they seem to be saying.

By learning to shift our focus from the content of our thoughts to being aware of our thoughts, we advance on the path of freedom from unhappiness.

The faster we cure our unawareness with regards to the words we speak, the words we hear, the things we see, and the thoughts in our mind, the faster we will be able to learn the art of being aware in the present moment.

Questions for contemplation

1. Contemplate and write down the situations when you tend to be unaware about what you say, hear, see, or think.

   _____

   _____

2. Contemplate and write down the steps you plan to take to break the vicious cycle of unawareness and to raise awareness.

   _____

   _____

13

Round-up Expectations of Help
The Best Help is Self-help

"No one helps when the time comes."
"Where is my family now that I need them?!"
"What useless neighbors I have! They are absolutely of no help at all."
"Of course, I don't have it. Whatever I need, I never seem to have."
"It has to rain when I am not carrying an umbrella!"

It is common to hear such complaints. Whenever you find yourself saying these words, contemplate on which one of the following statements seems more correct:

People do not help when required.

or

I don't help myself when required.

Whenever we feel that we are not receiving the help that we expect from others, we should first contemplate whether we are helping ourselves first. When we reflect on this, we will realize that many a time, we are not able to help ourselves.

Once this realization dawns, we must introspect what is it that we are doing that stops us from helping ourselves. Are we doing something that is proving to be counterproductive during times of need?

When we do not receive the help that we expect from others, we are gripped by negative thoughts. Very often, we lose our temper as well. We spend a lot of time obsessing over the negativity that fills our presence like poison. This negativity proves to be counterproductive and we are unable to step up and help ourselves. It is ironic that we criticize others for being unhelpful when we ourselves are being the same! Not only do we *not* help ourselves, but also spread negativity to others, causing unhappiness in their lives too.

To be free from such tendencies, we must round-up our expectations of receiving help from others and begin helping ourselves. Let us understand this with the help of an example:

Let's say we've decided to meditate for twenty minutes daily, but for some reason we're not able to complete the full twenty minutes of meditation every day. Sometimes we receive a call from the workplace, sometimes visitors show up, sometimes we're in the midst of some work and forget to meditate for the day—the reason can vary.

But when people call us, visit us, or give us tasks to complete, do we hold them responsible for our not being able to meditate? If we're doing so, then we're indulging in a blaming pattern. This is tantamount to us expecting them to help us meditate. Instead, if we were to find workarounds like meditating later at night or earlier in the day before starting work, we'll be helping ourselves.

Furthermore, the very thought that we failed to practice meditation today, makes us unhappy and blinds us from finding workarounds to improve the situation. Hence, we must first be thankful for whatever we are able to do. Gratitude inspires happiness, and happiness brings about growth.

Whenever we feel dejected about not receiving the expected help from certain people, we should understand that not getting help from a few people does not mean that the whole universe has forsaken us. There are so many people who are helping us—unseen and unknown to us. With Nature working in our favor, expecting help from others is not only unnecessary, but also a folly!

Every element in our life is always helping us in the right way. The trees around us are supporting us by synthesizing the oxygen we breathe, the ground that we walk on is supporting us. Our body is supporting us every second in ways hardly known to us. It is only when we have a nagging muscle spasm or physiological disorder that we realize how our body was working like a song!

The truth is that the entire universe is helping us, at every step, in every moment, with every breath. It's just that we need to have the eye to see it. We are so very engrossed in counting our problems that we forget to count our blessings!

Sometimes we commit the mistake of wasting time in expecting help from others. When our expectations are not met, we feel let down and deeply unhappy about having wasted our time. Further, we keep thinking, "If only I had done something myself, I could have been better off today." However, indulging in repentance is a further waste of time. At times, not receiving any help is the best help we can get! Such situations spur us into action and make us independent, confident, and are instrumental in making us learn something new.

Some people remain unhappy all their life because of things that they consider as their shortcomings. They suffer from a deep feeling of injustice, as if something irreversibly bad has happened to them. By remaining unhappy in this manner, they arrest their own ability to help themselves in rising up from their limitations. To be able to help themselves, they have to be happy first because it is their happiness that will bring about the much-needed success in their endeavors.

The world is replete with stories of several physically challenged people, who could overcome their disabilities and become independent. They were able to move ahead in life and serve as an inspiration for others—even those who are physically capable!

Louis Kuhne was a renowned German naturopath, who discovered unique natural ways of healing a wide spectrum of diseases, especially with the use of water. When Louis fell severely ill, he did not sit expecting help from others. Instead, he deepened his study and discovered novel ways to heal himself. With time, his expertise grew and benefitted several people around the world.

Likewise, we too, need to change our attitude. When we do not receive help from others, we should take charge of the situation ourselves. Whenever we are able to rise up to the occasion and help ourselves, we should also remember to thank ourselves for the emergence of the right response from within us.

By rounding-up the habit of expecting help from others, we begin to learn that only we can help ourselves the best and the most!

Questions for contemplation

1. Since your childhood, on which occasions have you felt that people haven't helped you the way you expected them to?
   _____
   _____

2. Contemplate and write down the negative thoughts that come to your mind on feeling disappointed by others.
   _____
   _____

3. Contemplate the same incidents in the light of the understanding you have today. Do you still think that people did not help you, or were *you* not able to help *yourself*? Write down your contemplation.
   _____
   _____

4. Contemplate and write down what you intend to do from now on, to be able to help yourself.
   _____
   _____

14

Round-up the Ego

Respect Yourself

We like to be respected, acknowledged, appreciated, and feel welcomed. We expect others to receive us well and attend to us, wherever we go. It makes us feel important.

We tend to dislike people who are stubborn, who won't agree with us, who seem to ignore us. We like to be with only those people who agree with us, who do our bidding. We like going only to those places where we are well-received and feel welcomed, even if the place is not right for us. Places where we do not feel welcome, do not attract us, however beneficial they may be.

People frequent gambling and liquor dens because they feel welcomed there; but they stay away from holy and spiritual places because their cravings are not fulfilled there. To get attention and importance from friends, they often get carried away and indulge in self-harming addictions. They feel happy when they are given attention, however, this happiness is only short lived.

When we contemplate, we begin to see this as the play of the ego. It is a requirement of the ego to feel welcomed, to feel respected, and to feel honored. It constantly craves for attention and feels momentarily satisfied only when this craving *appears to be* fulfilled.

However, trying to satisfy this craving for attention is like pouring oil into fire. The fire keeps growing and never really gets extinguished. Our goal is to annihilate the ego; to overcome the expectation of respect, love, and attention from others, and to learn self-respect.

The ignorance of the ego makes it blind to the difference between *self-respect* and *attention-from-others*. It does not know what it means to truly respect oneself; hence, it mistakes *attention-from-others* to be *self-respect*.

In order to satisfy their cravings for attention and respect, some people even indulge in gossip, or spreading confidential information about people. They feel that doing so will make people want to talk to them and respect them.

However, one needs to understand that such methods cannot be employed to earn respect. Whatever one receives in return for gossip and negative indulgences cannot be called '*respect*'! The annihilation of the ego begins when one learns to find within him whatever he was seeking outside. By doing this one gets rid of the unhappiness that comes from not getting respect and attention from others.

Those, who truly have self-respect, do not pay heed to the cravings of their ego. They do not make the mistake of going to places that dent their self-respect.

True love and respect can be experienced only in giving, not in seeking and expecting. People who exist in our lives are not here to love and respect us. They are here to remind us that we are the source of love and attention.

Logical reasoning suggests that we can get something only when we seek it outside us. We believe that we can experience love and self-respect only when we get it from others. However illogical as it may sound, the experience of pure love and true self-respect does not lie in getting, but rather in giving unconditionally. If we receive it back, it is merely a bonus.

True love, by nature, is giving. It gives boundlessly when it is brimming in life. Everything we see and experience is the expression of love. When we experience true love, we only feel like giving overwhelmingly and unconditionally. It feels great to expect nothing in return!

However, without knowing this, most people spend their entire lifetime seeking love and attention. Due to this fallacy, they keep yearning for appreciation, for consideration, for approval from others.

For example, someone, who has worked hard all through his work life and never received any appreciation, breaks down in tears when his office staff speak good things about him at his farewell. He has waited all those years to hear a few words of praise and approval. Not being aware of how true love and respect can be experienced, he keeps seeking them in the external world.

We can never find true and everlasting love and self-respect in the external world. Whenever we find ourselves feeling deprived of love and attention, we need to remind ourselves about this truth. By knowing that we are the source of love, we can love ourselves, instead of waiting to receive love from the world.

Ask yourself: "Why do I need an *agent* to love myself?" Waiting for the world to love you, is like hiring an agent to love yourself! When you love and respect yourself, your mere presence will radiate happiness to others. You won't feel the need to seek happiness, you will spread it!

Questions for contemplation

1. Contemplate on the incidents when you have felt unhappy because of the lack of respect, appreciation, attention, or love from others.

   _____

   _____

2. What mistakes have you made owing to the desire to feel appreciated or respected, for which you had to repent later?

   _____

   _____

3. Contemplate and write down the situations in which your desire to get attention from others intensifies.

   _____

   _____

4. How strong is your self-respect? In which particular situations do you feel the lack of true self-respect?

   _____

   _____

15

Deceit is a Disease
Innocence is a Virtue

Have you ever wondered why children are so lovable? It's due to the divine quality of innocence that is innately felt in their presence.

However, as they grow, their innocence gets shrouded by layers of negative programming and prejudices as their mind gets 'trained' and the ego steps in. Their original nature becomes increasingly dormant as deceit and shrewdness take over. They resort to manipulation and cunning to fulfil their desires. Without realizing it, they move away from their original nature of divine innocence.

Day by day, we succumb to the burden of negative thoughts, thus inviting several illnesses. Unhappiness and dissatisfaction keep increasing. This proves to be costly in the context of our life purpose.

Since childhood, we are taught by those around us, to be smart and sharp, the underlying belief being that if we are not, people will take us for a ride.

To fulfil our worldly desires, we start increasingly deviating from our innate qualities like love, joy, peace, and innocence. We are unaware of how much we lose as compared to how little we gain by this deviation.

Even if one were to achieve literally everything one desires at the cost of innocence, it would still be an unfortunate deal, for the benefits would only be short lived, but the losses almost permanent!

Many of us may not be convinced about this, but almost all our actions today are tainted by thoughts of deceit, greed, desires, jealousy, and resentment, which is why the results they garner are far from perfect.

Here's how it works: if a small error is introduced in the function of a calculator, whatever calculations it does thereafter—whether big or small—the results shall be skewed and far from perfect. Likewise, negative thoughts are like the basal error in our functioning and anything that results from there, will be imperfect.

Being innocent does not mean being naive, immature, or ignorant. Innocence is a state of inner purity, guilelessness, and natural integrity. It is a state uncorrupted by negative thoughts, prejudices, and conditioning of the past. This state only comes from the understanding of one's true nature beyond the body and mind.

Children are always in the natural state of being the true Self. They do not identify themselves as a boy, a girl, a son, a daughter, a brother, a sister, and so on. For them, the experience of their body and physical surroundings has not yet obscured the experience of the true Self, which is why innocence comes to them naturally. Innocence is a quality of the true Self. We link the word innocence with children because they live a life that is untainted by negative thoughts. The mere utterance of the word 'innocent' brings to mind a sweet, smiling, blissful face.

We begin losing our innocence when we start giving in to defilements such as anger, deceit, greed, lust, etc. This does not mean that *not* expressing these defilements is a proof of innocence. One could externally feign innocence but internally be afflicted with these vices. Conversely, one may express their feelings openly but be pure and sinless like an innocent child.

If you were to snatch a kid's toy, he or she might cry, scream, or even throw tantrums. But you wouldn't call such a kid bad-tempered or selfish, because as soon as you give back its toy, it is back to its original state. The kid won't have any aversions about you for having taken something from him. He won't harbor any hatred or seek revenge because the mind of the child is yet untainted by such negative conditioning.

While this state is innate for a child, it does not mean it is unachievable for us adults. One of the most effective ways to restore our innocence is to practice meditation. The goal of meditation is to empty the clutter that shrouds the experience of the true Self. When the clutter of past conditioning is eradicated, we return to the experience of the true Self and begin to abide in it.

With the practice of meditation, we begin the inward journey; all our conditioning begins to dissolve in the bright, divine light of the Self. As the conditioning disappears and the ego is annihilated, we return to our original state beyond thoughts—the state that children experience all the time; the state that we ourselves have experienced when we were children.

With the constant and sincere practice of meditation, we can rediscover the virtue of innocence, not just for a few moments, but for life.

Have you ever seen a sleeping child and thought how innocent and peaceful they look when they are asleep? But do children lose their innocence once they wake up? No! There is no negativity in them, and the negativity in the world that surrounds them, does not affect their innocence.

Similarly, it is possible for us to be aware and simultaneously unaware of the negativity in the world. Meaning, we can be aware of the negativity that appears to exist in the world around us, but it wouldn't affect our innocence.

It is true that children are constantly in the experience of the true Self, but they are not consciously aware that what they are experiencing is their true nature. In other words, children have the experience but not the wisdom. However, as adults, we can delve deep within and consciously experience the Self, distinct from the experience of our physical body. In other words, we are capable of both experience and wisdom. We can perceive our physical form and our true nature as two distinct experiences. When we meditate, we return to experiencing the Self, the way we did when we were kids; our innocence is restored in this state.

But as soon as we emerge from meditation, matters of the material world surround us, related thoughts, tendencies, and beliefs, all come rushing in, slowly obscuring the experience that we had during meditation. The ultimate state of meditation is when we always remain in the experience of the Self, while we go through our daily activities. This is also termed as 'Self-stabilization'.

We experience unhappiness because we have strayed away from our innocence. With the practice of meditation, we can realize our true nature and re-discover our innocence. The innocence of a child exists in everyone; all it needs is the removal of the mask of deceit.

Deceit may give us short term benefits, but we have to pay the price for our actions sooner or later. By paying close attention to our everyday activities, we can find out whether our actions are deceitful or genuine. How do we respond to people and situations? How do we interact with others? If we want something from someone, or want to get some work done, how do we get them to do it?

If we find any deceit in our behavior, we should raise our awareness about the underlying desires that cause us to act deceitfully in the first place and dispel them.

It is only by leading a deceit-free life that we can re-discover the happiness of our childhood and lead a life full of innocence. The time has come to round-up the negativities spread by deceit and become free from them.

Questions for contemplation

1. Which incidents in your life remind you of your innocence?

2. Recollect and introspect incidents when you resorted to deceit to fulfill your desires.

3. Contemplate and write down if you can remember, when, during your growing days, did you lose your innocence?

4. What steps do you plan to take to re-discover and sustain your innocence?

5. Write down your contemplation on how your life would be, after you have re-discovered your innocence.

16

Round-up Miserliness

Recognize the Opportunity of Sowing Positive Seeds

The ability of Nature to augment and multiply is one of its greatest blessings. We all have, at some point in our lives, experienced the joy of witnessing a seed sprout into a sapling after having sown it in soil. This is what Nature does—it nurtures seeds that are well sown and grows them, augments them, multiplies them. However, the key action here is the sowing of the seed.

It is as if Nature is eagerly waiting to reward us with a multiplied yield. But Nature can only do its part if we do ours. And the best way to do that is to take every opportunity to freely and abundantly sow seeds of positivity, wherever we can and however we can.

Offering money or efforts as a help to those in need, helping people solve their problems, helping someone get a job, giving someone time and listening to them, etc., are some examples of how we can get started. There are several positive and helpful things we can do wherever we are right now. We just have to realize the opportunities and turn them into seeds.

Nature's work is unseen

When the seed is sown, whatever happens with it in the soil is unseen. It is only when the plant grows out of the soil that we get to actually witness Nature's work. There are different types of seeds one can sow to grow different types of trees and plants.

Similarly, in the case of metaphorical seeds of positivity, there are several types of those too. Sincere appreciation, financially helping someone, taking efforts to serve, advising or consoling someone and praying for them, are all seeds! We are unaware of the form these seeds will take in our future. But as soon as we understand the way Nature works—how it nurtures the seeds, multiplies and manifests them—we begin to sow the right seeds plentifully and become free from miserliness and misery.

When a farmer sows seeds in his field, he does not upturn the soil every day to check whether the seeds have germinated or not. He has faith in the working of Nature which happens in the unseen.

The ill-effects of miserliness

A miser always feels good about his own miserliness because he thinks that by being a miser, he has "saved" a lot of things. However, when he considers the negative effects of miserliness in his life, he begins to realize the great price he is paying in return for the little "savings" he thought he was making. This realization frees him from his miserliness.

Someone may think that by holding on to their resources (like money, time, intelligence, skills, etc.) and not sharing them with others, they are "saving" their resources. The reason for not sharing is mostly the fear of running out of resources. It could also be a feeling of unworthiness of the receiver, or a sense of exclusive entitlement. Either way, by not sharing their resources, they are unconsciously choosing to not sow seeds.

A miser feels good about "saving money" by not buying a return ticket when he sees that his boat is sinking! His desperate eagerness to hang on to what he has, makes him blind to the greater misfortune that is headed his way!

By not sowing positive seeds of faith, the miser unknowingly sows seeds of misery. In a family, even if one of the family members is a miser, it negatively affects all the other family members. They have to face a lot of difficulties. As a result, peace in the family is disrupted. If the miser could see this and become aware, there is a better chance that he might take steps to change his conduct. The understanding that whatever one gives away is a seed, not a waste, helps here.

Miserliness can also spread from one person to another like a contagious disease. Every person that one comes in contact with frequently, influences him in some way. Therefore, people who come in constant contact with misers tend to be subconsciously influenced by them and resort to miserliness, ending up disadvantaging themselves. Here's a small story that is a joke, but also serves as an example of how one person's miserliness spreads to others.

> A miser once donated his blood to a very rich man. When the rich man recovered from his illness, he gifted the miser with a car. The miser was naturally ecstatic at having received such a 'pricey' gift for something that was supposed to be a donation.
>
> A few years rolled by and once again, the rich man was in need of blood. The miser eagerly volunteered to donate blood once again, with the expectation of receiving an even bigger gift this time. When the rich man recovered, he gifted the miser a box of sweets.
>
> Disappointed by what he had received, the miser said to the rich man, "Sir, the last time I gave you blood, you gifted me a car; and this time……" The rich man smiled, "Yes, after all, I have a miser's blood flowing in my veins!"

This was just a joke, but this little story is a humorous representation of how miserliness spreads from one person to another; how the thoughts of people who come in contact with a miser get influenced.

The miserly way of thinking is, "By giving, we lose and by receiving, we gain," "If I give what I have, I will lose what I had." This thought will never let a person give away anything to anyone. The understanding should be: **The more I give, the better I receive! Everything I give is a seed.**

Prayer is a seed too

Help offered to others doesn't always have to be in the form of money, efforts or time. There are several people who do not have these resources but are eagerly willing to help others. Such people should know that they can still help people by using the resources of time and attention.

Prayer is a great seed too. Praying to God, to Nature, or to one's Guru, for the wellbeing and progress of others, for the betterment of all mankind, is a great way to help and sow seeds of positivity for oneself. One can even pray for specific people who are in need. Having prayed, one has to keep faith in Nature's working and let it do its part.

Every seed has the potential of creating a forest. No matter how small the seed, it has the ability to create miracles.

Sow seeds in happiness

Every action we perform has a distinct feeling associated with it. Love, joy, and peace are feelings that all of us ultimately seek. However, it is a mistake to seek these emotions outside ourselves. Happiness is not the outcome of any event; it is a choice we have to make every moment. Thus, happiness is not the desired outcome; it is the factor that precipitates the desired outcome.

When we sow seeds, the feeling with which we sow them is the most important aspect. When we sow seeds of positivity with happiness, the happiness catalyzes and improves the quality of the harvest. In fact, our feelings are the real seeds. More than what we give, what matters is with what feeling we give. We harvest the seeds of the feelings that we sow.

It is hence very important to sow seeds with happiness. When we offer alms to a beggar, we should not be thinking, *"Here goes a few bucks that I will never see again!"* The understanding should be, *"I am not giving this to the beggar. This is my contribution to Nature's work."* This understanding will help the seed germinate. Hence, we have to sow seeds in the right soil, with the right feeling, and the right understanding.

Nature wants us to sow as many seeds as we can, so that it may multiply them and return to us. So, with whatever we have today, let us give the best that we can. Even having positive thoughts for someone is a seed.

Finally, while we sow the seeds of positivity by helping others, we have to sow seeds for ourselves too by having a positive, compassionate, loving, forgiving, and respectful attitude towards ourselves.

How many times have we said to ourselves, "I like you the way you are; I respect you the way you are; I forgive you no matter what"? How many times do we thank our body—every part from the head to the toe—for making it possible to experience life and for being the greatest help in achieving our life purpose on Earth? It is time we did all of that.

Do not exercise any restraint when loving yourself, thanking yourself, and saying positive things about yourself. Do it with open arms, an open mind, and an open heart, for the more you thank, the more you get!

Let us experience a beautiful and healthy life and also become an inspiration for others to lead a better life. Let us sow seeds of positivity and witness the awesomeness of Nature with wonder!

Questions for contemplation

1. When and in which matters have you been miserly till date?
   _____
   _____

2. What steps would you plan to take to overcome any miserliness?
   _____
   _____

3. Have you gone out of your way to help someone in need? What help did you render?
   _____
   _____

4. In how many different ways can you sow seeds for Nature to work upon?
   _____
   _____

5. How do you think a prayer seed can help?
   _____
   _____

6. I resolve to sow these seeds daily (Write this down in your diary):
   a._____ f._____
   b._____ g._____
   c._____ h._____
   d._____ i._____
   e._____ j._____

17

Negligence is a Disease

Mindfulness is the Cure

There once lived in a village, a person by the name of Marc. He was quite ill-famed in the village as a person whose bad dreams always turned out to be true.

If there was a wedding in the village, he would have a dream in which the wedding procession got attacked by dacoits. If there was a housewarming ceremony, he would have a dream in which the new house would catch fire. When his dreams started coming true, the superstitious villagers drove him out of the village.

Feeling dejected, Marc travelled to a nearby town and got a job as a night guard in the king's army. A few days later, when the king was scheduled to visit a nearby kingdom, Marc had a dream in which that kingdom was hit by an earthquake.

The next day, as the king's entourage approached the gate to leave for the other kingdom, Marc hesitatingly approached the king and requested an audience with him. Upon being allowed, he told the king about the previous night's dream and urged the king to cancel his visit if possible.

For some reason, the king heeded his words and cancelled the trip. The following day, the king was shocked to hear that the kingdom he was to visit was indeed hit by a severe earthquake causing great destruction and deaths. Shocked but pleased at being saved from an unfortunate accident, the king called for Marc. He gave him great rewards for saving his life but also fired him from his job!

The firing of Marc from his job by the king may come as a surprise to you, but if you think about it, you will find it a justified act. Marc was employed as a night guard, who shouldn't have slept on duty! Wakefulness was the first and most important requirement of his job, and he had failed at it. His negligence lost him his job.

Marc's story gives us something to think about: are we wakeful and aware about what happens to us? Every day, as we go about our tasks, are we present in the moment or are we lingering in the stories of the past or the imaginations of the future?

Different people are at different levels of awareness. Some people are completely unaware about their state and surroundings. They live their lives in utter ignorance. Others continue doing their work as if they are doing some menial task not bothering about the quality of the work or ever thinking about improving it. Such people lead a life of apathetic indifference. And then there are those who put all their mind, heart, and awareness in their work without thinking about gains. They dedicate every action to God, offering every *karma* as a service unto God. It is not very hard to imagine which category of people end up leading a better and happier life.

The present is called the '*present*' because it is the greatest gift we have and will ever need. Mindfulness in the present moment, in the present action, in the present situation is the key to eternal happiness and satisfaction. It is also the door to enter the timeless space within. Neither the past nor the future is capable of giving such pure and everlasting happiness, and yet unfortunately we spend a lot of energy on them.

We cannot 'think' about the present, the way we do about the past and the future. We can only *be* in the present. This *being* is who we truly are. These moments that we are present in, just being, are when we are truly alive. It is these precious moments that make our lifetime worthwhile; and it is these very moments that most of us squander away in our preoccupation with the dead past and non-existent future.

Questions for contemplation

1. When and why do you get distracted by the past or the future?

   _____

   _____

2. What steps do you plan to take to improve your mindfulness in the present moment?

   _____

   _____

18

Accept Your Parcels

Plant the Seeds of Positive Feelings

There are four ways or four planes on which we respond to any incident: feelings, thoughts, speech, and action. The foremost corner is that of feelings. If this response is controlled, all the others are automatically taken care of and life becomes pleasant and effortless.

Our feelings control our thoughts, and our thoughts have a great impact on our speech and actions. Hence, by sowing the right seeds of feelings, we take care of all four at the same time.

Let us understand this with some examples.

Incident 1:

Imagine you are hosting a party at home and have invited some friends over. Suddenly, you happen to notice one of your friends pick up a currency note lying on the mantelpiece and quietly slip it into his pocket.

Contemplate how you would feel about the situation and particularly your friend.

Incident 2:

Suppose you are walking through the marketplace. You get your wallet out to pay for something and accidentally drop a currency note down. Before you realize what has happened, an unknown person rushes forth from the crowd, picks up the note, and makes away with it.

Contemplate what your feelings would be in this situation. Contemplate the difference in your feelings between the first and second incidents.

Incident 3:

You are playing with your pet dog, and accidentally drop a currency note on the floor. The dog snatches the note away, tearing it, before you can pick it up.

Incident 4:

You are walking on the road, counting the money in your wallet. Just then, a strong breeze blows and a note flies away.

Now, which of the four incidents will trouble you the most and the least. Note that in each incident, you incur the same loss, and yet your feelings in each case are different. In each incident, you sow different seeds of feelings.

If you were selling your farm to someone, would you sow seeds in the farm before selling it? No. You would tell the purchaser, "The field is now yours; it is up to you to sow the seeds of your choice."

Similarly, Nature has given us this fertile field of life in which we can grow health, wealth, relationships, skills, just about anything; but Nature hasn't sown any seeds in it. Had it given us the field with seeds already sown in it, we would have said, "I am left with no choice but to accept the seeds that have already been sown!" But, that's not how Nature works. Everyone has the freedom of choice. We choose the seeds we want to sow.

Let's say we do not sow any seeds in our field for a long time. What's the worst that could happen? You might say, "At the worst, the field will lay barren for as long as we don't sow seeds in it." But that is not true. We know that an uncultivated field gets infested by poisonous weeds and thorny shrubs. Snakes and scorpions invade such a land, moving freely through the wild growth.

In much the same way, by not sowing positivity in the field of life that Nature has bestowed upon us, we invite the infestation of the poisonous weeds of negative thoughts. In our ignorance, we keep sowing negative seeds, thus reaping sorrow and pain. These negative seeds are sown through our feelings, thoughts, speech, and actions. As we have seen, out of the four, the seeds that are sown by our feelings are the most potent.

Going back to the four hypothetical situations in which you lose the same amount of money, in which one of those situations would you sow the most negative seeds?

Naturally, the first incident, which involved a close friend of yours, would arouse the strongest negative feelings like hatred and disgust. If he were never to admit his theft and apologize for his behavior, you would feel even more negative. These feelings of hatred, disgust and unhappiness that we entertain, are the seeds we sow.

To stop sowing such negative seeds, we must always choose to have positive feelings, whatever be the situation. Choosing a positive attitude in every situation is an art, which can be learnt with the right understanding and proper practice.

The understanding should be that whatever happens to us, whatever comes to us—be it positive, negative, profit, loss, good, bad, elevating, depressing—is sent by Nature. These are parcels sent by Nature.

In all the four incidents, we lose the same amount of money, whoever or whatever the reason for the loss may be. The understanding in this particular situation should be that losing the money—the actual incident—was the parcel that Nature intended to send us. Whoever or whatever turns out to be the medium to deliver the parcel is immaterial. Our task is to accept the parcel gracefully; i.e., recognize and learn the lesson that Nature has sent for us.

It may appear that different mediums were responsible for the loss each time, but the fact is that Nature takes the help of different mediums to send us our parcels, our lessons.

While accepting the parcels—whether positive or negative—we need to understand that it is *our* parcel, which we were meant to receive. Nature has chosen some medium—a person, an animal, or a situation—to deliver the parcel to us. However, this does not mean that the medium is responsible for it. The medium is only serving as a courier to deliver the parcel to us. We have to open the parcel gracefully and retrieve our lesson.

However, in the absence of this understanding, we accuse the people delivering the parcel of being responsible for it and reject the parcel; in other words, we refuse to learn the lesson that was meant for us in the situation. As a result of this misunderstanding, we direct our negative feelings towards people and thus sow the wrong seeds of negative feelings. The outcome is that similar negative parcels keep repeating in our life. The lesson we are supposed to learn, comes to us in different ways till we stop rejecting it and learn it.

It is therefore imperative for us to be aware while receiving our parcels. We need to accept them happily and gracefully without sowing negative seeds. We need to be vigilant of the feelings that we allow to arise within us in response to incidents.

This necessarily means that no one else is responsible. Every incident is *our* parcel sent by Nature and the ideal response from us is to accept it happily and gracefully, learn the right lesson, and thus sow the right seeds for the future.

Questions for contemplation

1. Which seeds of feelings have you sown so far? Contemplate and pen down your findings?

   _____

   _____

2. Which seeds of feelings do you intend to sow, now that you have the right understanding and awareness?

   _____

   _____

3. With the understanding that you have gained, how will you perceive the parcels received from Nature, hereafter?

   _____

   _____

19

Round-up Acquisition and Preservation

Find Happiness in the Present Moment

Most people spend all their lives focusing on acquiring for the future and preserving whatever was acquired in the past. In doing so, they are lost to the happiness of the present moment. Instead of focusing on what they have *now*, they focus either on what they had in the past or desire for the future. Focusing on something they do not have now, will naturally bring unhappiness and dissatisfaction.

People run the rat race of life, thinking about satisfying some desire all the time. They cannot feel peaceful until their desires are fulfilled; but the chain of desires is unending. With the fulfilment of one desire, they may experience peace and happiness for a short period. But almost immediately, another one takes its place, and the rat race continues. This cycle of acquisition and preservation troubles people all their lives.

You may have heard people say, "Last year's New Year eve was far more enjoyable than this year!" Some may remark, "Last year, my business was booming; this year it's just not as good!"

The mind always sacrifices the joy of the present moment to preserve whatever it has acquired in the past or to acquire what it desires in the future. Some people may have experienced that they are feeling happy and positive in one moment, and then suddenly they remember something of the past, which they don't have any more or something they desire in the future that they do not currently have. So, they instantly feel sad in the very next moment.

During such times, we should become aware of exactly what is happening with us. We stray away from the joy of the present moment, engaging in the thoughts of acquiring and preserving. With this awareness, our focus should return to the center of the line that joins preservation and acquisition—the present moment. This is possible only when we become aware about the thoughts that drift us away from the aliveness that we feel in the present.

A successful sculptor was once asked about how he went about creating masterpieces; what his process was. The sculptor replied, "It is very simple. If I am making a statue of the Buddha, I begin with a block of stone and I simply chisel away everything that is *not* the Buddha. What remains is the Buddha!"

Likewise, when we successfully remove all unwanted thoughts (thoughts of acquiring, preserving, desires etc.) the bliss that was enshrouded behind these thoughts emerges.

Even though a sculptor is working with a block of stone, his focus is on the form that the stone has to take. We too have to focus on the joy that lies beyond the pull of the past and future, beyond acquiring and preserving. Whatever is unnecessary will automatically drop off. We do not have to resist or eliminate the thoughts of acquiring or preserving; we just have to eliminate the effect they have on us; the unhappiness and dejection they cause us. By doing so, the impact of the tendency of acquiring and preserving, automatically dissolves.

The troubles we are experiencing today indicate that our focus is on the stone and not the form it is supposed to take. When the stone takes the final form, meaning when we are able to focus on the joy of the present moment, without dabbling in the past or the future, we experience the dissolution of this habit of acquiring and preserving.

Questions for contemplation

1. Notice the times when you indulge in acquiring and preserving at the cost of enjoying the present moment. How much trouble have you faced due to this tendency? Write down your contemplation.

_____

_____

20

Round-up Your Fears and Tendencies
Learn Your Earth Lessons

If we were to carefully analyze the people we are surrounded by, we will notice they all have specific behavioral patterns, particular fears, and certain set ways in which they respond to events in their lives.

Applying the same careful analysis to ourselves will also reveal these aspects within us. Some of these patterns develop over years and are a result of conscious or unconscious conditioning that our mind goes through, to a point where our responses are almost automatic.

On the other hand, certain patterns or fears may be unexplainable, but they are present all the same since our childhood. These are injured memories—negative memories that need healing. They are implanted in us at birth.

As a simple example, if an injured memory of a drowned death is placed in a person, the person experiences fear of water, fear of drowning, fear of sea travel, etc. These fears seem unexplainable because there is no logical reason for the person to have the fear of water. The fear has its root in the injured memory placed in the person. It is the person's responsibility to face these fears and overcome them, to learn his lessons and heal the injured memory.

Our existence on earth has a particular purpose. We are all here to learn certain lessons. The lessons, of course, change from person to person. For some, the lesson is to control their anger; for some the lesson is empathy, and for someone, the lesson might be to learn the value of relationships. There are several profound lessons that can be listed. We all have many lessons to learn during our existence here on earth. We can consider this as a syllabus that is set for every person.

However, there is one lesson that is a part of every one's syllabus. It is the one lesson, the one quality that can only be understood and learnt here on earth, and is hence probably the most important reason for our existence here.

What lesson could this be? What could be the one thing that is common to all our syllabuses?

Patience!

We are all here to learn patience and get trained at it. Nearly everything we want to do here on Earth, requires us to be patient. Think about it. A person wants to become a doctor, or an engineer or a painter. He has to be patient; he has to take lessons, then he has to practice. He may even have to face failures and get better at being perseverant before he achieves his goal. The underlying lesson remains: patience.

Someone who wants to get rich has to make plans, set goals, decide upon an action plan, and finally be patient! A person suddenly wakes up at night and is not able to go back to sleep. Instead of worrying, he has to be patient until he feels sleepy again.

This lesson even applies to the spiritual realm. A person wants to be happy in every situation. He has to be patient while he understands the essence of happiness before he can actually practice and perfect the art of being happy all the time, no matter what!

In short, everything that happens with us is trying to teach us a lesson. Just like a teacher who has to repeat lessons if a child is not able to learn, Nature will keep scripting similar events again and again, until we buckle down and learn our lessons.

If you have noticed that similar incidents keep happening with you again and again in different ways and probably through different people, there is definitely a lesson for you to learn. The moment you realize this and learn the lesson, the events stop recurring.

But how do we recognize what our lessons are? How can a person know for certain whether or not a certain virtue is his lesson?

This is where things get a bit subtle. The answer to this question can only be arrived at by each individual by themselves. The way to do that is through self-observation and introspection.

One of the best and most straightforward ways to realize what your lessons are is to find out what you are bad at; what you are not able to do easily.

For example:

- For a person who finds it difficult to control his anger in situations, learning to be calm and grounded is the lesson.
- For someone who finds it difficult to give things away, generosity is the lesson.
- For one who finds it difficult to understand people, to understand their feelings and perspectives, empathy is the lesson.
- For a person who has any fear (like the fear or heights, fire, closed spaces, water, crowds, etc.) the lesson would be to muster courage and overcome the fear by confronting it.
- For those who finds it difficult to trust people, faith and trustworthiness are their lessons.
- For someone who get easily irritated and despises others, the lesson is of compassion.

The beauty of Nature is that it supports us in every way in learning our lessons. The people, things and situations that we are surrounded by are a part of an immaculate system put in place by Nature to help us learn our lessons. If our lesson is to overcome anger, we will be surrounded by people who constantly provoke our anger. Incidents that make us angry will keep repeating until we realize and learn our lesson. If our lesson is kindness and generosity, we will face people and incidents where we have to give things away.

It is hence imperative for us to observe our patterns and focus on those things that we find difficult instead of focusing on things that we are already good at. For example, if we have healthy relationships, we need not work on our relationship skills; we are already good at it. We should instead find something that we are *not* good at.

An effective way to get started can be to analyze the whole day before going to sleep at night. Go through everything that happened to you from the moment you woke up till the moment you settled down for the night. Separate out incidents that are pertaining to your particular lesson(s) and analyze whether or not your response was appropriate. If it was not, make a mental note of it and resolve to respond differently the next time. The next night, analyze if you were able to respond differently in at least one or two such incidents. This daily ritual can help you disintegrate deep patterns, learn your lessons, and transform your life.

Finally, the greatest arrow in every spiritual warrior's quiver is prayer. Pray for release from your negative and destructive patterns. Praying helps channelize your energy in the direction that you want to progress. With prayer, you can attune yourself with Nature. The more you attune yourself with nature, the more you begin to realize that everything—literally everything—around you is constantly helping you achieve your life purpose!

Questions for contemplation

1. Which behavioral patterns, fears, and beliefs are you able to bring to light through introspection?

   _____

   _____

2. In which situations do your fears, beliefs, or tendencies overcome you? Introspect and write down the situations, so that you may become more aware of them when they recur and avoid repeating your past reactions.

   _____

   _____

3. Contemplate and write down how your life will be after you have rounded up all your behavioral patterns, false beliefs, and fears?

   _____

   _____

21

The Art of Contemplation
Re-thinking and Focused Writing

Having considered the various aspects of life that we need to introspect and work upon, it is time that we commence the exercise of deep contemplation. This chapter discusses the nuances and significance of contemplation and gives pointers on how we can go about the process.

Most people tend to follow a fixed pattern of daily life. However, the factors that govern our lives keep changing over time. As a result, the situations or factors that influenced our decisions earlier may no longer apply today.

There is always room for improvement, fine tuning, and re-orientation in whatever we do. Hence, we need to take a pause and re-think. We need to determine whether we should continue to follow the same course of action that we have been doing till date, or will it merit to make suitable course corrections.

Re-thinking our life challenges us to think out-of-box. It is essential to take stock of subtle and gradual changes that happen around us. Using this approach, we can make appropriate changes within us.

There are two kinds of people: those who never re-think their lives, and those who do so regularly. The former group keep repeating past mistakes and encounter failures in life. The second set of people contemplate such questions as: How can I enhance my future performance? What mistakes did I make, and what were the positive highlights of the year?

Of course, we need not wait for the end of the calendar year to introspect; we can do it between two events. After one task is complete and before beginning the next one, we can take advantage of the opportunity to re-think.

For example, between the time when a student completes his annual examinations and when the exam results are posted, he can avail himself of the time gap to contemplate his plan for further studies in the next academic year. He can ask himself: What mistakes did I make this term? Which is my favorite subject? Which subject does not interest me? How can I make further progress in my studies during the vacation? Students can mull over many such questions depending on their specific needs. If a student performs such introspection, very soon he will excel in academics.

Taking time out to contemplate our life is not a time to sulk over the mistakes of the past, but rather to learn from them and stride towards creating a brighter future. We should resolve to learn from our mistakes, and not repeat them. Such contemplation can help us shape a brilliant future.

The Power of Contemplation

Many people are not used to introspecting and consider it a waste of time. But once they give it a try and begin to notice the changes taking place within them, they soon begin to see contemplation as an excellent opportunity. Without it, diamonds remain mere pieces of coal. Contemplation is the process of cutting through the coal to reveal the hidden diamonds within.

Contemplation is not just about thinking; it has to be followed by action. Until we start acting upon the subject of our contemplation, it remains incomplete. Without action, contemplation is unfinished; without contemplation, actions are blind and directionless.

When we gain a thorough understanding through contemplation, our thoughts automatically begin to shape our actions. For example, after we contemplate the benefits of keeping our books in order on the bookshelf, we will naturally begin to keep them well-organized. If we do not begin placing them systematically after the period of contemplation, it indicates a weakness in the quality of our contemplation.

During the period of contemplation, we begin to realize that we know far too little about ourselves. We will then pay attention to our thought processes, our behavior patterns and tendencies, and make appropriate changes within.

Contemplation is the most effective way of bringing the unseen to light. When we are able to grasp the invisible truths of our life, we can make remarkable progress. If we wish to move ahead, it is imperative that the unseen be brought to light.

Many of us understand the importance of contemplation but do not practice it. We may even avoid contemplation due to procrastination and short-sightedness. We tend to think, "Everything is going well today; so, there's no need to contemplate. I can always do it later." Then tomorrow brings challenges for which we are unprepared, because we failed to contemplate the day before.

We need to decide NOW to get out of this self-defeating cycle. We have to undertake contemplation and follow up with actions. Therefore, we should ask ourselves the following three key questions:

1. What will I gain through contemplation?
2. Do I really want what I can gain through contemplation?
3. Am I ready to make the necessary changes that my contemplation might suggest?

The answers to these three questions will provide you with powerful motivation. Let us consider these questions in detail.

The first question is: What will I gain through contemplation?

Do we clearly know what we stand to gain from effective contemplation? Unaware of its potential benefits, we are not sufficiently motivated to begin. Before beginning to contemplate, we must first think: "What will I get upon contemplating?" Upon contemplating and performing actions in the right way, several positive changes can take place:

- We can attain our goal in life.
- We can get rid of our wrong habits and tendencies.
- We can enhance our higher qualities.
- We can manage time effectively and implement changes in the present, keeping the future in mind.
- Our relationships can be improved.
- Through right planning, we can overcome our financial concerns.
- We can progress in our spiritual journey
- We can dissolve all the complaints that keep nagging us today.

In this way, we can transform our entire life with the help of effective contemplation.

Now, let's investigate the second question: Do I really want what I can gain through contemplation?

Often man's words and actions lack coordination. One may say, "I want to progress... I want to be successful... I want to bring about changes in my life and grow," and so on. But when it is time to act, one hangs back. One feels the need to move ahead, but he is not prepared for it.

The second question really calls for a deeper introspection into whether we really yearn for the benefits contemplation can give us. This question should not be merely answered in words, but from the heart, from our innermost core. If we are able to alter our actions, then we can progress further; otherwise we need to re-think the first question.

The answer to the second question must arise from our inner conviction. This conviction will emerge only when we are sincere in our resolve to reach our goal. A strong resolve will help us stay focused on the path of progress. Hence, it is very important to answer it honestly.

Now let us look at the third question: Am I ready to make the changes that my contemplation might suggest?

This question is linked to the second. If you have answered the second question positively, then the answer to the third one will be straight forward. The third question leads you directly to action. You should tread the path of contemplation only when you are genuinely prepared for transforming yourself.

Many a times we say, "I want to translate my thoughts into action," but due to wrong habits of the body like laziness and indiscipline, we are unable to do so. Our contemplation should gain such depth that it immediately leads to action.

Contemplation gathers depth and direction when it is backed by the habit of focused writing.

Focused Writing – an effective tool

When we are not used to the practice of focused writing, it may seem trivial to us. We may find it unnecessary. But as soon as we start practicing this sincerely and regularly, we will find that it serves as a catalyst for inner transformation and re-inventing ourselves.

Focused writing helps us realize our perspective towards our life. Those who write their diary consistently with a vision are bound to see transformation in their lives. The habit of focused writing also acts as a feedback mechanism for us.

When we start writing down whatever occurs to our mind, it makes it possible to encounter our deep-seated limiting beliefs and negative emotions that lie suppressed within us. When they are brought to light, it makes it possible to release them and break free.

Focused writing also enables us to develop the art of contemplation. When we try to contemplate mentally, our thoughts can fool us. When conflicting thoughts arise, without being observed and audited, they can lead us in unwanted directions, leading us to false conclusions. Focused writing helps us audit and observe our own thoughts in a detached manner.

The following tips can be helpful to practice the art of focused writing:

- During the course of a day, we can learn a lot from the way we handle situations and deal with people. But in due course of time, we tend to forget what we had learned. Every night before going to bed, it helps to reflect on lessons learned during the day and jot them down in our diary.

- Very often, people who write their diary do not follow a system of writing. Due to this, they forget what they had written, where and when. Hence, we should develop our own system for writing our diary. We may use a paper diary or notebook, a computer-based journal, or a mobile app.

- It is not necessary to write down elaborate sentences in the diary. We may write short and precise points using keywords that can help reproduce and remember everything at a later date.

- With the passage of time, it is necessary to consistently keep looking out for items that can be removed or updated based on new lessons learned or new ideas.

- We should write down the positive qualities or strengths that we have noticed in people around us. We should also read them regularly. This helps in reducing our weaknesses and creating a bright future.

- It is important to regularly read what we have written in our diary.

A diamond's true worth is known only after it is cut. Prior to that, a diamond is nothing but an ordinary stone. A jeweler cuts it and bestows it with its true identity. Similarly, when you walk the path of progress through contemplation, you will shine like a diamond. From this will emerge your higher, more evolved nature; a nature you have hidden within you since many years!

● ● ●

You can mail your opinion or feedback on this book to:
books.feedback@tejgyan.org

About Sirshree

Sirshree's spiritual quest, which began during his childhood, led him on a journey through various schools of philosophy and meditation practices. He studied a wide range of literature on mind science and spirituality. After a long period of deep contemplation on the truth of life, his quest culminated in attaining the ultimate truth.

Sirshree espouses, "All spiritual paths that lead to the truth begin differently but culminate at the same point – Understanding. This understanding is complete in itself. Listening to this understanding is enough to attain the Truth." Over the last two decades, he has dedicated his life to raising mass consciousness.

Sirshree has delivered more than 4000 discourses that throw light on this understanding. He has designed a system for wisdom, which makes it accessible to all. This system has inspired people from all walks of life to progress on their journey of the Truth. Thousands of seekers join in a virtual prayer for World Peace and Global Healing daily at 9:09 am and 9:09 pm.

About Tej Gyan Foundation

Tej Gyan Foundation is a non-profit organization founded on the teachings of Sirshree. The Foundation disseminates Tejgyan – the wisdom that guides one from self-development to Self-realization, leading towards Self-stabilization.

The Foundation's system for imparting wisdom has been assessed by international quality auditors and accredited with the ISO 9001:2015 certification. This wisdom has been presented in a simple, systematic, and practically applicable form that makes it accessible to people from all walks of life, regardless of religion, caste, social strata, country, or belief system.

The Foundation has centers in more than 400 cities and towns across India and other countries. The mission of Tej Gyan Foundation is to create a highly evolved society by leading seekers from negative to positive thoughts and further, from positive thoughts to Happy thoughts. A 'Happy thought' is the auspicious thought of being free from all thoughts, leading to the state of supreme bliss beyond thoughts.

If you seek such wisdom that leads you beyond mere knowledge, dissolves all problems, frees you from all limiting beliefs, reveals the true nature of divinity, and establishes you in the ultimate truth, then it is time to discover Tejgyan; it is time to rise above the mundane knowledge of words and experience Tejgyan!

The MahaAasmani Magic of Awakening Retreat

Self-development to Self-realization towards Self-stabilization

Do you wish to experience unconditional happiness that is not dependent on any reason? Happiness that is permanent and only increases with time? Do you wish to experience love, peace, self-belief, harmony in relationships, prosperity, and true contentment? Do you wish to progress in all facets of your life, viz. physical, mental, social, financial, and spiritual?

If you seek answers to these questions and are thirsty for the ultimate truth, then you are welcome to participate in the MahaAasmani Magic of Awakening retreat organized by Tej Gyan Foundation. This is the Foundation's flagship retreat based on the teachings of Sirshree.

The Purpose of this Retreat

The purpose of this retreat is that every human being should:

- Discover the answer to "Who am I" and "Why am I?" through direct experience and be established in ultimate bliss.

- Learn the art of living in the present, free from the burden of the past and the anxiety of the future.

- Acquire practical tools to help quieten the chattering mind and dissolve problems.

- Discover missing links in the practices of Meditation (*Dhyana*), Action (*Karma*), Wisdom (*Gyana*), and Devotion (*Bhakti*).

About Books by Sirshree

Sirshree's published work includes more than 150 book titles, some of which have been translated into more than 10 languages. His literature provides a profound reading on various topics of practical living and unravels the missing links in karma, wisdom, devotion, meditation, and consciousness.

His books have been published by leading publishing houses like Penguin, Hay House, Bloomsbury, Wisdom Tree, Jaico, etc. "The Source" book series, authored by Sirshree, has sold over 10 million copies. Various luminaries and celebrities like His Holiness the Dalai Lama, publishers Mr. Reid Tracy, Ms. Tami Simon and Yoga Master Dr. B. K. S. Iyengar have released Sirshree's books and lauded his work.

The Source
Attain Both, Inner Peace
and Worldly success

Awaken the Power of Faith
Discover the 7 Principles of the
Highest Power of the Universe

To order books authored by Sirshree, login to:
www.gethappythoughts.org
For further details, call: +91 9011013210

SELECT BOOKS AUTHORED BY SIRSHREE

   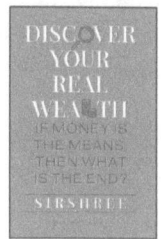

 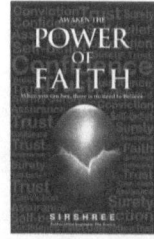  

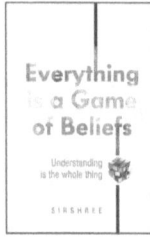   

To order these and other books authored by Sirshree
Visit **www.gethappythoughts.org**

Tej Gyan Foundation – Contact details

Registered Office:
Happy Thoughts Building, Vikrant Complex, Near Tapovan Mandir, Pimpri, Pune 411017, INDIA. Contact: +91 20-27411240, +91 20-27412576

MaNaN Ashram:
Survey No. 43, Sanas Nagar, Nandoshi Gaon, Kirkatwadi Phata, Off Sinhagad Road, Taluka Haveli, Pune district - 411024, INDIA. Contact: +91 992100 8060.

WORLD PEACE PRAYER

Divine Light of Love, Bliss, and Peace is Showering;
The Golden Light of Higher Consciousness is Rising;
All negativity on Earth is Dissolving;
Everyone is in Peace and Blissfully Shining;
O God, Gratitude for Everything!

Members of Tej Gyan Foundation have been offering this impersonal mass prayer for many years. Those who are happy can offer this prayer. Those feeling low or suffering from illness can receive healing with this prayer.

If you are feeling troubled or sick, please sit to receive the healing effect of this prayer. Visualize that the divine white healing light is being showered on earth through the prayers of thousands and is also reaching you, bringing you peace and good health. You can dwell in this feeling for some time and then offer your gratitude to those offering the prayer.

A Humble Appeal

More than a million peace lovers are praying for World Peace and Global Healing every morning and evening at 9:09. This prayer is also webcast on YouTube at 9:00 pm. Please participate in this noble endeavor.

www.ingramcontent.com/pod-product-compliance
Lightning Source LLC
LaVergne TN
LVHW040155080526
838202LV00042B/3177